THIS LOG BOOK BELONGS TO

NAME
ADDRESS
TEL.

I LOVE MY FISH!

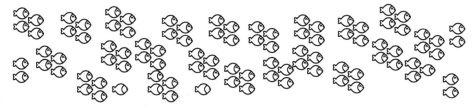

DATE

TIME

TANK

WATER TYPE

WATER QUALITY

• TEMP	• % CHANGE
• PH LEVEL	• AMMONIA
• NITRITE	• NITRATE

FISH COUNT

FISHES ADDED

FISHES LOST

FISH BEHAVIOUR

LAZY 1   2   3   4   5 ACTIV

AQUARIUM CHECK LIST

GEAR / EQUIPMENT	TICK BOX	ADDITIONAL NOTES
• FILTERS CHECKED?	☐	
• PUMPS CHECKED?	☐	
• TUBING CHECKED?	☐	
• NET CHECKED?	☐	
• LIGHTING CHECKED?	☐	
• WATER LEVEL CHECKED?	☐	
• CONDITIONER CHECKED?	☐	
• HEATER CHECKED?	☐	

ADDITIONAL NOTES

AQUASCAPE IDEAS & SKETCHES

DATE

TIME

TANK

WATER TYPE

WATER QUALITY

• TEMP	• % CHANGE
• PH LEVEL	• AMMONIA
• NITRITE	• NITRATE

FISH COUNT

FISHES ADDED

FISHES LOST

FISH BEHAVIOUR

LAZY 1 2 3 4 5 ACTIVE

AQUARIUM CHECK LIST

GEAR / EQUIPMENT	TICK BOX	ADDITIONAL NOTES
FILTERS CHECKED?	☐	
PUMPS CHECKED?	☐	
TUBING CHECKED?	☐	
NET CHECKED?	☐	
LIGHTING CHECKED?	☐	
WATER LEVEL CHECKED?	☐	
CONDITIONER CHECKED?	☐	
HEATER CHECKED?	☐	

ADDITIONAL NOTES

AQUASCAPE IDEAS & SKETCHES

📅 **DATE**	◌ **WATER QUALITY**	
🕐 **TIME**	• TEMP	• % CHANGE
🐠 **TANK**	• PH LEVEL	• AMMONIA
🌊 **WATER TYPE**	• NITRITE	• NITRATE

🐟 **FISH COUNT**
🐠 **FISHES ADDED**
🐟 **FISHES LOST**

FISH BEHAVIOUR

🐠   1   2   3   4   5   🐟
LAZY ◯   ◯   ◯   ◯   ◯ ACTIV

AQUARIUM CHECK LIST

🔧 GEAR / EQUIPMENT	☑ TICK BOX	📝 ADDITIONAL NOTES
• FILTERS CHECKED?	☐	
• PUMPS CHECKED?	☐	
• TUBING CHECKED?	☐	
• NET CHECKED?	☐	
• LIGHTING CHECKED?	☐	
• WATER LEVEL CHECKED?	☐	
• CONDITIONER CHECKED?	☐	
• HEATER CHECKED?	☐	

ADDITIONAL NOTES	**AQUASCAPE IDEAS & SKETCHES**

DATE

TIME

TANK

WATER TYPE

WATER QUALITY

• TEMP	• % CHANGE
• PH LEVEL	• AMMONIA
• NITRITE	• NITRATE

FISH COUNT

FISHES ADDED

FISHES LOST

FISH BEHAVIOUR

| LAZY | 1 ○ | 2 ○ | 3 ○ | 4 ○ | 5 ○ | ACTIVE |

AQUARIUM CHECK LIST

GEAR / EQUIPMENT	TICK BOX	ADDITIONAL NOTES
FILTERS CHECKED?	☐	
PUMPS CHECKED?	☐	
TUBING CHECKED?	☐	
NET CHECKED?	☐	
LIGHTING CHECKED?	☐	
WATER LEVEL CHECKED?	☐	
CONDITIONER CHECKED?	☐	
HEATER CHECKED?	☐	

ADDITIONAL NOTES

AQUASCAPE IDEAS & SKETCHES

📅 DATE	
🕐 TIME	
🐠 TANK	
〰️ WATER TYPE	

WATER QUALITY

• TEMP	• % CHANGE
• PH LEVEL	• AMMONIA
• NITRITE	• NITRATE

🐟 FISH COUNT	
🐟 FISHES ADDED	
🐟 FISHES LOST	

FISH BEHAVIOUR

LAZY 🐟   1   2   3   4   5   🐟 ACTIVE

AQUARIUM CHECK LIST

🔧 GEAR / EQUIPMENT	☑️ TICK BOX	📝 ADDITIONAL NOTES
• FILTERS CHECKED?	☐	
• PUMPS CHECKED?	☐	
• TUBING CHECKED?	☐	
• NET CHECKED?	☐	
• LIGHTING CHECKED?	☐	
• WATER LEVEL CHECKED?	☐	
• CONDITIONER CHECKED?	☐	
• HEATER CHECKED?	☐	

ADDITIONAL NOTES

AQUASCAPE IDEAS & SKETCHES

DATE

TIME

TANK

WATER TYPE

WATER QUALITY

• TEMP	• % CHANGE
• PH LEVEL	• AMMONIA
• NITRITE	• NITRATE

FISH COUNT

FISHES ADDED

FISHES LOST

FISH BEHAVIOUR

LAZY 1 2 3 4 5 ACTIVE

AQUARIUM CHECK LIST

GEAR / EQUIPMENT	TICK BOX	ADDITIONAL NOTES
FILTERS CHECKED?	☐	
PUMPS CHECKED?	☐	
TUBING CHECKED?	☐	
NET CHECKED?	☐	
LIGHTING CHECKED?	☐	
WATER LEVEL CHECKED?	☐	
CONDITIONER CHECKED?	☐	
HEATER CHECKED?	☐	

ADDITIONAL NOTES

AQUASCAPE IDEAS & SKETCHES

| 📅 **DATE** |
| 🕐 **TIME** |
| 🐠 **TANK** |
| 〰️ **WATER TYPE** |

💧 WATER QUALITY

• TEMP	• % CHANGE
• PH LEVEL	• AMMONIA
• NITRITE	• NITRATE

| 🐟 **FISH COUNT** |
| 🐠 **FISHES ADDED** |
| 🐟 **FISHES LOST** |

FISH BEHAVIOUR

🐠   1 —— 2 —— 3 —— 4 —— 5   🐟
LAZY ○   ○   ○   ○   ○ ACTIV

AQUARIUM CHECK LIST

🛠️ GEAR / EQUIPMENT	☑️ TICK BOX	✏️ ADDITIONAL NOTES
• FILTERS CHECKED?	☐	
• PUMPS CHECKED?	☐	
• TUBING CHECKED?	☐	
• NET CHECKED?	☐	
• LIGHTING CHECKED?	☐	
• WATER LEVEL CHECKED?	☐	
• CONDITIONER CHECKED?	☐	
• HEATER CHECKED?	☐	

ADDITIONAL NOTES

AQUASCAPE IDEAS & SKETCHES

DATE

TIME

TANK

WATER TYPE

WATER QUALITY

• TEMP	• % CHANGE
• PH LEVEL	• AMMONIA
• NITRITE	• NITRATE

FISH COUNT

FISHES ADDED

FISHES LOST

FISH BEHAVIOUR

LAZY   1   2   3   4   5   ACTIVE

AQUARIUM CHECK LIST

GEAR / EQUIPMENT	TICK BOX	ADDITIONAL NOTES
FILTERS CHECKED?	☐	
PUMPS CHECKED?	☐	
TUBING CHECKED?	☐	
NET CHECKED?	☐	
LIGHTING CHECKED?	☐	
WATER LEVEL CHECKED?	☐	
CONDITIONER CHECKED?	☐	
HEATER CHECKED?	☐	

ADDITIONAL NOTES

AQUASCAPE IDEAS & SKETCHES

DATE

TIME

TANK

WATER TYPE

WATER QUALITY

• TEMP	• % CHANGE
• PH LEVEL	• AMMONIA
• NITRITE	• NITRATE

FISH COUNT

FISHES ADDED

FISHES LOST

FISH BEHAVIOUR

LAZY 1   2   3   4   5 ACTIVE

AQUARIUM CHECK LIST

GEAR / EQUIPMENT	TICK BOX	ADDITIONAL NOTES
• FILTERS CHECKED?	☐	
• PUMPS CHECKED?	☐	
• TUBING CHECKED?	☐	
• NET CHECKED?	☐	
• LIGHTING CHECKED?	☐	
• WATER LEVEL CHECKED?	☐	
• CONDITIONER CHECKED?	☐	
• HEATER CHECKED?	☐	

ADDITIONAL NOTES

AQUASCAPE IDEAS & SKETCHES

DATE

TIME

TANK

WATER TYPE

WATER QUALITY

• TEMP	• % CHANGE
• PH LEVEL	• AMMONIA
• NITRITE	• NITRATE

FISH COUNT

FISHES ADDED

FISHES LOST

FISH BEHAVIOUR

LAZY 1 2 3 4 5 ACTIVE

AQUARIUM CHECK LIST

GEAR / EQUIPMENT	TICK BOX	ADDITIONAL NOTES
FILTERS CHECKED?	☐	
PUMPS CHECKED?	☐	
TUBING CHECKED?	☐	
NET CHECKED?	☐	
LIGHTING CHECKED?	☐	
WATER LEVEL CHECKED?	☐	
CONDITIONER CHECKED?	☐	
HEATER CHECKED?	☐	

ADDITIONAL NOTES

AQUASCAPE IDEAS & SKETCHES

DATE

TIME

TANK

WATER TYPE

WATER QUALITY

• TEMP	• % CHANGE
• PH LEVEL	• AMMONIA
• NITRITE	• NITRATE

FISH COUNT

FISHES ADDED

FISHES LOST

FISH BEHAVIOUR

LAZY 1 2 3 4 5 ACTIVE

AQUARIUM CHECK LIST

GEAR / EQUIPMENT	TICK BOX	ADDITIONAL NOTES
• FILTERS CHECKED?	☐	
• PUMPS CHECKED?	☐	
• TUBING CHECKED?	☐	
• NET CHECKED?	☐	
• LIGHTING CHECKED?	☐	
• WATER LEVEL CHECKED?	☐	
• CONDITIONER CHECKED?	☐	
• HEATER CHECKED?	☐	

ADDITIONAL NOTES

AQUASCAPE IDEAS & SKETCHES

DATE

TIME

TANK

WATER TYPE

WATER QUALITY

• TEMP	• % CHANGE
• PH LEVEL	• AMMONIA
• NITRITE	• NITRATE

FISH COUNT

FISHES ADDED

FISHES LOST

FISH BEHAVIOUR

LAZY 1 2 3 4 5 ACTIVE

AQUARIUM CHECK LIST

GEAR / EQUIPMENT	TICK BOX	ADDITIONAL NOTES
FILTERS CHECKED?	☐	
PUMPS CHECKED?	☐	
TUBING CHECKED?	☐	
NET CHECKED?	☐	
LIGHTING CHECKED?	☐	
WATER LEVEL CHECKED?	☐	
CONDITIONER CHECKED?	☐	
HEATER CHECKED?	☐	

ADDITIONAL NOTES

AQUASCAPE IDEAS & SKETCHES

📅 DATE		💧 **WATER QUALITY**	
🕐 TIME		• TEMP	• % CHANGE
🐟 TANK		• PH LEVEL	• AMMONIA
🌊 WATER TYPE		• NITRITE	• NITRATE

🐠 FISH COUNT
🐟 FISHES ADDED
🐟 FISHES LOST

FISH BEHAVIOUR

🐟 LAZY 1 ○ 2 ○ 3 ○ 4 ○ 5 ○ ACTIV 🐟

AQUARIUM CHECK LIST

🔧 GEAR / EQUIPMENT	☰ TICK BOX	📝 ADDITIONAL NOTES
• FILTERS CHECKED?	☐	
• PUMPS CHECKED?	☐	
• TUBING CHECKED?	☐	
• NET CHECKED?	☐	
• LIGHTING CHECKED?	☐	
• WATER LEVEL CHECKED?	☐	
• CONDITIONER CHECKED?	☐	
• HEATER CHECKED?	☐	

ADDITIONAL NOTES	**AQUASCAPE IDEAS & SKETCHES**

DATE

TIME

TANK

WATER TYPE

WATER QUALITY

• TEMP	• % CHANGE
• PH LEVEL	• AMMONIA
• NITRITE	• NITRATE

FISH COUNT

FISHES ADDED

FISHES LOST

FISH BEHAVIOUR

LAZY 1 2 3 4 5 ACTIVE

AQUARIUM CHECK LIST

GEAR / EQUIPMENT	TICK BOX	ADDITIONAL NOTES
FILTERS CHECKED?	☐	
PUMPS CHECKED?	☐	
TUBING CHECKED?	☐	
NET CHECKED?	☐	
LIGHTING CHECKED?	☐	
WATER LEVEL CHECKED?	☐	
CONDITIONER CHECKED?	☐	
HEATER CHECKED?	☐	

ADDITIONAL NOTES

AQUASCAPE IDEAS & SKETCHES

📅 **DATE**	
🕐 **TIME**	
🐟 **TANK**	
🌊 **WATER TYPE**	

💧 WATER QUALITY

• TEMP	• % CHANGE
• PH LEVEL	• AMMONIA
• NITRITE	• NITRATE

🐠 **FISH COUNT**
🐟 **FISHES ADDED**
🐟 **FISHES LOST**

FISH BEHAVIOUR

🐠 LAZY 1 ◯ 2 ◯ 3 ◯ 4 ◯ 5 ◯ ACTIV 🐟

AQUARIUM CHECK LIST

🔧 GEAR / EQUIPMENT	📋 TICK BOX	📝 ADDITIONAL NOTES
• FILTERS CHECKED?	☐	
• PUMPS CHECKED?	☐	
• TUBING CHECKED?	☐	
• NET CHECKED?	☐	
• LIGHTING CHECKED?	☐	
• WATER LEVEL CHECKED?	☐	
• CONDITIONER CHECKED?	☐	
• HEATER CHECKED?	☐	

ADDITIONAL NOTES

AQUASCAPE IDEAS & SKETCHES

DATE

TIME

TANK

WATER TYPE

WATER QUALITY

• TEMP	• % CHANGE
• PH LEVEL	• AMMONIA
• NITRITE	• NITRATE

FISH COUNT

FISHES ADDED

FISHES LOST

FISH BEHAVIOUR

LAZY 1 2 3 4 5 ACTIVE

AQUARIUM CHECK LIST

GEAR / EQUIPMENT	TICK BOX	ADDITIONAL NOTES
FILTERS CHECKED?	☐	
PUMPS CHECKED?	☐	
TUBING CHECKED?	☐	
NET CHECKED?	☐	
LIGHTING CHECKED?	☐	
WATER LEVEL CHECKED?	☐	
CONDITIONER CHECKED?	☐	
HEATER CHECKED?	☐	

ADDITIONAL NOTES

AQUASCAPE IDEAS & SKETCHES

📅 **DATE**	💧 **WATER QUALITY**	
🕐 **TIME**	• TEMP	• % CHANGE
🐠 **TANK**	• PH LEVEL	• AMMONIA
〰 **WATER TYPE**	• NITRITE	• NITRATE

🐟 **FISH COUNT**
🐟 **FISHES ADDED**
🐟 **FISHES LOST**

FISH BEHAVIOUR

🐟 LAZY 1 ◯ 2 ◯ 3 ◯ 4 ◯ 5 ◯ ACTIVE 🐟

AQUARIUM CHECK LIST

🔧 GEAR / EQUIPMENT	☑ TICK BOX	✍ ADDITIONAL NOTES
• FILTERS CHECKED?	☐	
• PUMPS CHECKED?	☐	
• TUBING CHECKED?	☐	
• NET CHECKED?	☐	
• LIGHTING CHECKED?	☐	
• WATER LEVEL CHECKED?	☐	
• CONDITIONER CHECKED?	☐	
• HEATER CHECKED?	☐	

ADDITIONAL NOTES

AQUASCAPE IDEAS & SKETCHES

DATE	**WATER QUALITY**	

DATE

TIME

TANK

WATER TYPE

WATER QUALITY

• TEMP	• % CHANGE
• PH LEVEL	• AMMONIA
• NITRITE	• NITRATE

FISH COUNT

FISHES ADDED

FISHES LOST

FISH BEHAVIOUR

	1	2	3	4	5	
LAZY	○	○	○	○	○	ACTIVE

AQUARIUM CHECK LIST

GEAR / EQUIPMENT	TICK BOX	ADDITIONAL NOTES
FILTERS CHECKED?	☐	
PUMPS CHECKED?	☐	
TUBING CHECKED?	☐	
NET CHECKED?	☐	
LIGHTING CHECKED?	☐	
WATER LEVEL CHECKED?	☐	
CONDITIONER CHECKED?	☐	
HEATER CHECKED?	☐	

ADDITIONAL NOTES

AQUASCAPE IDEAS & SKETCHES

📅 DATE		💧 WATER QUALITY	
🕐 TIME		• TEMP	• % CHANGE
🐠 TANK		• PH LEVEL	• AMMONIA
〰️ WATER TYPE		• NITRITE	• NITRATE

🐟 FISH COUNT	
🐟 FISHES ADDED	
🐟 FISHES LOST	

FISH BEHAVIOUR

🐠 LAZY 1 — 2 — 3 — 4 — 5 🐟 ACTIV
○ ○ ○ ○ ○

AQUARIUM CHECK LIST

🔧 GEAR / EQUIPMENT	📋 TICK BOX	📝 ADDITIONAL NOTES
• FILTERS CHECKED?	☐	
• PUMPS CHECKED?	☐	
• TUBING CHECKED?	☐	
• NET CHECKED?	☐	
• LIGHTING CHECKED?	☐	
• WATER LEVEL CHECKED?	☐	
• CONDITIONER CHECKED?	☐	
• HEATER CHECKED?	☐	

ADDITIONAL NOTES

AQUASCAPE IDEAS & SKETCHES

DATE

TIME

TANK

WATER TYPE

WATER QUALITY

• TEMP	• % CHANGE
• PH LEVEL	• AMMONIA
• NITRITE	• NITRATE

FISH COUNT

FISHES ADDED

FISHES LOST

FISH BEHAVIOUR

LAZY ◯ 1 ◯ 2 ◯ 3 ◯ 4 ◯ 5 ACTIVE

AQUARIUM CHECK LIST

GEAR / EQUIPMENT	TICK BOX	ADDITIONAL NOTES
FILTERS CHECKED?	☐	
PUMPS CHECKED?	☐	
TUBING CHECKED?	☐	
NET CHECKED?	☐	
LIGHTING CHECKED?	☐	
WATER LEVEL CHECKED?	☐	
CONDITIONER CHECKED?	☐	
HEATER CHECKED?	☐	

ADDITIONAL NOTES

AQUASCAPE IDEAS & SKETCHES

📅 DATE		⬡ WATER QUALITY	
🕐 TIME		• TEMP	• % CHANGE
🐟 TANK		• PH LEVEL	• AMMONIA
🌊 WATER TYPE		• NITRITE	• NITRATE

🐠 FISH COUNT
🐟 FISHES ADDED
🐟 FISHES LOST

FISH BEHAVIOUR

🐟 1   2   3   4   5 🐟

LAZY ○   ○   ○   ○   ○ ACTIV

AQUARIUM CHECK LIST

🔧 GEAR / EQUIPMENT	☑ TICK BOX	📝 ADDITIONAL NOTES
• FILTERS CHECKED?	☐	
• PUMPS CHECKED?	☐	
• TUBING CHECKED?	☐	
• NET CHECKED?	☐	
• LIGHTING CHECKED?	☐	
• WATER LEVEL CHECKED?	☐	
• CONDITIONER CHECKED?	☐	
• HEATER CHECKED?	☐	

ADDITIONAL NOTES

AQUASCAPE IDEAS & SKETCHES

DATE

TIME

TANK

WATER TYPE

WATER QUALITY

• TEMP	• % CHANGE
• PH LEVEL	• AMMONIA
• NITRITE	• NITRATE

FISH COUNT

FISHES ADDED

FISHES LOST

FISH BEHAVIOUR

LAZY 1 2 3 4 5 ACTIVE

AQUARIUM CHECK LIST

GEAR / EQUIPMENT	TICK BOX	ADDITIONAL NOTES
FILTERS CHECKED?	☐	
PUMPS CHECKED?	☐	
TUBING CHECKED?	☐	
NET CHECKED?	☐	
LIGHTING CHECKED?	☐	
WATER LEVEL CHECKED?	☐	
CONDITIONER CHECKED?	☐	
HEATER CHECKED?	☐	

ADDITIONAL NOTES

AQUASCAPE IDEAS & SKETCHES

📅 **DATE**		◌ **WATER QUALITY**	
🕐 **TIME**		• TEMP	• % CHANGE
🐠 **TANK**		• PH LEVEL	• AMMONIA
〰 **WATER TYPE**		• NITRITE	• NITRATE

🐠 **FISH COUNT**
🐟 **FISHES ADDED**
🐟 **FISHES LOST**

FISH BEHAVIOUR

🐟 LAZY 1 ◯ 2 ◯ 3 ◯ 4 ◯ 5 ◯ ACTIV 🐟

AQUARIUM CHECK LIST

🔧 GEAR / EQUIPMENT	☰ TICK BOX	🖊 ADDITIONAL NOTES
• FILTERS CHECKED?	☐	
• PUMPS CHECKED?	☐	
• TUBING CHECKED?	☐	
• NET CHECKED?	☐	
• LIGHTING CHECKED?	☐	
• WATER LEVEL CHECKED?	☐	
• CONDITIONER CHECKED?	☐	
• HEATER CHECKED?	☐	

ADDITIONAL NOTES

AQUASCAPE IDEAS & SKETCHES

	DATE
	TIME
	TANK
	WATER TYPE

WATER QUALITY

• TEMP	• % CHANGE
• PH LEVEL	• AMMONIA
• NITRITE	• NITRATE

	FISH COUNT
	FISHES ADDED
	FISHES LOST

FISH BEHAVIOUR

LAZY 1 2 3 4 5 ACTIVE

AQUARIUM CHECK LIST

GEAR / EQUIPMENT	TICK BOX	ADDITIONAL NOTES
FILTERS CHECKED?	☐	
PUMPS CHECKED?	☐	
TUBING CHECKED?	☐	
NET CHECKED?	☐	
LIGHTING CHECKED?	☐	
WATER LEVEL CHECKED?	☐	
CONDITIONER CHECKED?	☐	
HEATER CHECKED?	☐	

ADDITIONAL NOTES

AQUASCAPE IDEAS & SKETCHES

DATE		WATER QUALITY	
TIME		• TEMP	• % CHANGE
TANK		• PH LEVEL	• AMMONIA
WATER TYPE		• NITRITE	• NITRATE

FISH COUNT
FISHES ADDED
FISHES LOST

FISH BEHAVIOUR

LAZY 1 2 3 4 5 ACTIV

AQUARIUM CHECK LIST

GEAR / EQUIPMENT	TICK BOX	ADDITIONAL NOTES
• FILTERS CHECKED?	☐	
• PUMPS CHECKED?	☐	
• TUBING CHECKED?	☐	
• NET CHECKED?	☐	
• LIGHTING CHECKED?	☐	
• WATER LEVEL CHECKED?	☐	
• CONDITIONER CHECKED?	☐	
• HEATER CHECKED?	☐	

ADDITIONAL NOTES

AQUASCAPE IDEAS & SKETCHES

DATE

TIME

TANK

WATER TYPE

WATER QUALITY

• TEMP	• % CHANGE
• PH LEVEL	• AMMONIA
• NITRITE	• NITRATE

FISH COUNT

FISHES ADDED

FISHES LOST

FISH BEHAVIOUR

LAZY 1   2   3   4   5 ACTIVE

AQUARIUM CHECK LIST

GEAR / EQUIPMENT	TICK BOX	ADDITIONAL NOTES
FILTERS CHECKED?	☐	
PUMPS CHECKED?	☐	
TUBING CHECKED?	☐	
NET CHECKED?	☐	
LIGHTING CHECKED?	☐	
WATER LEVEL CHECKED?	☐	
CONDITIONER CHECKED?	☐	
HEATER CHECKED?	☐	

ADDITIONAL NOTES

AQUASCAPE IDEAS & SKETCHES

DATE

TIME

TANK

WATER TYPE

WATER QUALITY

• TEMP	• % CHANGE
• PH LEVEL	• AMMONIA
• NITRITE	• NITRATE

FISH COUNT

FISHES ADDED

FISHES LOST

FISH BEHAVIOUR

LAZY   1   2   3   4   5   ACTIV

AQUARIUM CHECK LIST

GEAR / EQUIPMENT	TICK BOX	ADDITIONAL NOTES
• FILTERS CHECKED?	☐	
• PUMPS CHECKED?	☐	
• TUBING CHECKED?	☐	
• NET CHECKED?	☐	
• LIGHTING CHECKED?	☐	
• WATER LEVEL CHECKED?	☐	
• CONDITIONER CHECKED?	☐	
• HEATER CHECKED?	☐	

ADDITIONAL NOTES

AQUASCAPE IDEAS & SKETCHES

DATE		WATER QUALITY	
TIME		• TEMP	• % CHANGE
TANK		• PH LEVEL	• AMMONIA
WATER TYPE		• NITRITE	• NITRATE

FISH COUNT

FISHES ADDED

FISHES LOST

FISH BEHAVIOUR

LAZY 1 2 3 4 5 ACTIVE

AQUARIUM CHECK LIST

GEAR / EQUIPMENT	TICK BOX	ADDITIONAL NOTES
FILTERS CHECKED?	☐	
PUMPS CHECKED?	☐	
TUBING CHECKED?	☐	
NET CHECKED?	☐	
LIGHTING CHECKED?	☐	
WATER LEVEL CHECKED?	☐	
CONDITIONER CHECKED?	☐	
HEATER CHECKED?	☐	

ADDITIONAL NOTES

AQUASCAPE IDEAS & SKETCHES

DATE

TIME

TANK

WATER TYPE

WATER QUALITY

• TEMP	• % CHANGE
• PH LEVEL	• AMMONIA
• NITRITE	• NITRATE

FISH COUNT

FISHES ADDED

FISHES LOST

FISH BEHAVIOUR

LAZY 1 2 3 4 5 ACTIV

AQUARIUM CHECK LIST

GEAR / EQUIPMENT	TICK BOX	ADDITIONAL NOTES
• FILTERS CHECKED?	☐	
• PUMPS CHECKED?	☐	
• TUBING CHECKED?	☐	
• NET CHECKED?	☐	
• LIGHTING CHECKED?	☐	
• WATER LEVEL CHECKED?	☐	
• CONDITIONER CHECKED?	☐	
• HEATER CHECKED?	☐	

ADDITIONAL NOTES

AQUASCAPE IDEAS & SKETCHES

DATE		WATER QUALITY	
TIME		TEMP	% CHANGE
TANK		PH LEVEL	AMMONIA
WATER TYPE		NITRITE	NITRATE

FISH COUNT	FISH BEHAVIOUR
FISHES ADDED	
FISHES LOST	LAZY 1 2 3 4 5 ACTIVE

AQUARIUM CHECK LIST

GEAR / EQUIPMENT	TICK BOX	ADDITIONAL NOTES
FILTERS CHECKED?	☐	
PUMPS CHECKED?	☐	
TUBING CHECKED?	☐	
NET CHECKED?	☐	
LIGHTING CHECKED?	☐	
WATER LEVEL CHECKED?	☐	
CONDITIONER CHECKED?	☐	
HEATER CHECKED?	☐	

ADDITIONAL NOTES

AQUASCAPE IDEAS & SKETCHES

DATE

TIME

TANK

WATER TYPE

WATER QUALITY

• TEMP	• % CHANGE
• PH LEVEL	• AMMONIA
• NITRITE	• NITRATE

FISH COUNT

FISHES ADDED

FISHES LOST

FISH BEHAVIOUR

LAZY 1 2 3 4 5 ACTIVE

AQUARIUM CHECK LIST

GEAR / EQUIPMENT	TICK BOX	ADDITIONAL NOTES
• FILTERS CHECKED?	☐	
• PUMPS CHECKED?	☐	
• TUBING CHECKED?	☐	
• NET CHECKED?	☐	
• LIGHTING CHECKED?	☐	
• WATER LEVEL CHECKED?	☐	
• CONDITIONER CHECKED?	☐	
• HEATER CHECKED?	☐	

ADDITIONAL NOTES

AQUASCAPE IDEAS & SKETCHES

DATE

TIME

TANK

WATER TYPE

WATER QUALITY

• TEMP	• % CHANGE
• PH LEVEL	• AMMONIA
• NITRITE	• NITRATE

FISH COUNT

FISHES ADDED

FISHES LOST

FISH BEHAVIOUR

LAZY 1 2 3 4 5 ACTIVE

AQUARIUM CHECK LIST

GEAR / EQUIPMENT	TICK BOX	ADDITIONAL NOTES
FILTERS CHECKED?	☐	
PUMPS CHECKED?	☐	
TUBING CHECKED?	☐	
NET CHECKED?	☐	
LIGHTING CHECKED?	☐	
WATER LEVEL CHECKED?	☐	
CONDITIONER CHECKED?	☐	
HEATER CHECKED?	☐	

ADDITIONAL NOTES

AQUASCAPE IDEAS & SKETCHES

DATE

TIME

TANK

WATER TYPE

WATER QUALITY

• TEMP	• % CHANGE
• PH LEVEL	• AMMONIA
• NITRITE	• NITRATE

FISH COUNT

FISHES ADDED

FISHES LOST

FISH BEHAVIOUR

LAZY 1 2 3 4 5 ACTIV

AQUARIUM CHECK LIST

GEAR / EQUIPMENT	TICK BOX	ADDITIONAL NOTES
• FILTERS CHECKED?	☐	
• PUMPS CHECKED?	☐	
• TUBING CHECKED?	☐	
• NET CHECKED?	☐	
• LIGHTING CHECKED?	☐	
• WATER LEVEL CHECKED?	☐	
• CONDITIONER CHECKED?	☐	
• HEATER CHECKED?	☐	

ADDITIONAL NOTES

AQUASCAPE IDEAS & SKETCHES

DATE

TIME

TANK

WATER TYPE

WATER QUALITY

• TEMP	• % CHANGE
• PH LEVEL	• AMMONIA
• NITRITE	• NITRATE

FISH COUNT

FISHES ADDED

FISHES LOST

FISH BEHAVIOUR

LAZY   1   2   3   4   5   ACTIVE

AQUARIUM CHECK LIST

GEAR / EQUIPMENT	TICK BOX	ADDITIONAL NOTES
FILTERS CHECKED?	☐	
PUMPS CHECKED?	☐	
TUBING CHECKED?	☐	
NET CHECKED?	☐	
LIGHTING CHECKED?	☐	
WATER LEVEL CHECKED?	☐	
CONDITIONER CHECKED?	☐	
HEATER CHECKED?	☐	

ADDITIONAL NOTES

AQUASCAPE IDEAS & SKETCHES

DATE

TIME

TANK

WATER TYPE

WATER QUALITY

• TEMP	• % CHANGE
• PH LEVEL	• AMMONIA
• NITRITE	• NITRATE

FISH COUNT

FISHES ADDED

FISHES LOST

FISH BEHAVIOUR

LAZY 1 2 3 4 5 ACTIVE

AQUARIUM CHECK LIST

GEAR / EQUIPMENT	TICK BOX	ADDITIONAL NOTES
• FILTERS CHECKED?	☐	
• PUMPS CHECKED?	☐	
• TUBING CHECKED?	☐	
• NET CHECKED?	☐	
• LIGHTING CHECKED?	☐	
• WATER LEVEL CHECKED?	☐	
• CONDITIONER CHECKED?	☐	
• HEATER CHECKED?	☐	

ADDITIONAL NOTES

AQUASCAPE IDEAS & SKETCHES

DATE

TIME

TANK

WATER TYPE

FISH COUNT

FISHES ADDED

FISHES LOST

WATER QUALITY

· TEMP	· % CHANGE
· PH LEVEL	· AMMONIA
· NITRITE	· NITRATE

FISH BEHAVIOUR

LAZY   1   2   3   4   5   ACTIVE

AQUARIUM CHECK LIST

GEAR / EQUIPMENT	TICK BOX	ADDITIONAL NOTES
FILTERS CHECKED?	☐	
PUMPS CHECKED?	☐	
TUBING CHECKED?	☐	
NET CHECKED?	☐	
LIGHTING CHECKED?	☐	
WATER LEVEL CHECKED?	☐	
CONDITIONER CHECKED?	☐	
HEATER CHECKED?	☐	

ADDITIONAL NOTES

AQUASCAPE IDEAS & SKETCHES

📅 DATE		💧 WATER QUALITY	
🕐 TIME		• TEMP	• % CHANGE
🐟 TANK		• PH LEVEL	• AMMONIA
🌊 WATER TYPE		• NITRITE	• NITRATE

🐠 FISH COUNT
🐟 FISHES ADDED
🐟 FISHES LOST

FISH BEHAVIOUR

🐟 LAZY   1 ◯   2 ◯   3 ◯   4 ◯   5 ◯   ACTIV 🐟

AQUARIUM CHECK LIST

🔧 GEAR / EQUIPMENT	☑ TICK BOX	📝 ADDITIONAL NOTES
• FILTERS CHECKED?	☐	
• PUMPS CHECKED?	☐	
• TUBING CHECKED?	☐	
• NET CHECKED?	☐	
• LIGHTING CHECKED?	☐	
• WATER LEVEL CHECKED?	☐	
• CONDITIONER CHECKED?	☐	
• HEATER CHECKED?	☐	

ADDITIONAL NOTES

AQUASCAPE IDEAS & SKETCHES

DATE

TIME

TANK

WATER TYPE

WATER QUALITY

• TEMP	• % CHANGE
• PH LEVEL	• AMMONIA
• NITRITE	• NITRATE

FISH COUNT

FISHES ADDED

FISHES LOST

FISH BEHAVIOUR

LAZY 1 2 3 4 5 ACTIVE

AQUARIUM CHECK LIST

GEAR / EQUIPMENT	TICK BOX	ADDITIONAL NOTES
FILTERS CHECKED?	☐	
PUMPS CHECKED?	☐	
TUBING CHECKED?	☐	
NET CHECKED?	☐	
LIGHTING CHECKED?	☐	
WATER LEVEL CHECKED?	☐	
CONDITIONER CHECKED?	☐	
HEATER CHECKED?	☐	

ADDITIONAL NOTES

AQUASCAPE IDEAS & SKETCHES

DATE	WATER QUALITY

DATE

TIME

TANK

WATER TYPE

WATER QUALITY

• TEMP	• % CHANGE
• PH LEVEL	• AMMONIA
• NITRITE	• NITRATE

FISH COUNT

FISHES ADDED

FISHES LOST

FISH BEHAVIOUR

LAZY 1 2 3 4 5 ACTIV

AQUARIUM CHECK LIST

GEAR / EQUIPMENT	TICK BOX	ADDITIONAL NOTES
• FILTERS CHECKED?	☐	
• PUMPS CHECKED?	☐	
• TUBING CHECKED?	☐	
• NET CHECKED?	☐	
• LIGHTING CHECKED?	☐	
• WATER LEVEL CHECKED?	☐	
• CONDITIONER CHECKED?	☐	
• HEATER CHECKED?	☐	

ADDITIONAL NOTES

AQUASCAPE IDEAS & SKETCHES

DATE

TIME

TANK

WATER TYPE

WATER QUALITY

• TEMP	• % CHANGE
• PH LEVEL	• AMMONIA
• NITRITE	• NITRATE

FISH COUNT

FISHES ADDED

FISHES LOST

FISH BEHAVIOUR

LAZY 1 2 3 4 5 ACTIVE

AQUARIUM CHECK LIST

GEAR / EQUIPMENT	TICK BOX	ADDITIONAL NOTES
FILTERS CHECKED?	☐	
PUMPS CHECKED?	☐	
TUBING CHECKED?	☐	
NET CHECKED?	☐	
LIGHTING CHECKED?	☐	
WATER LEVEL CHECKED?	☐	
CONDITIONER CHECKED?	☐	
HEATER CHECKED?	☐	

ADDITIONAL NOTES

AQUASCAPE IDEAS & SKETCHES

📅 DATE		💧 WATER QUALITY	
🕐 TIME		• TEMP	• % CHANGE
🐟 TANK		• PH LEVEL	• AMMONIA
🌊 WATER TYPE		• NITRITE	• NITRATE

🐠 FISH COUNT	
🐟 FISHES ADDED	
🐟 FISHES LOST	

FISH BEHAVIOUR

🐟 LAZY   1   2   3   4   5   🐟 ACTIVE

AQUARIUM CHECK LIST

🔧 GEAR / EQUIPMENT	☑ TICK BOX	✏ ADDITIONAL NOTES
• FILTERS CHECKED?	☐	
• PUMPS CHECKED?	☐	
• TUBING CHECKED?	☐	
• NET CHECKED?	☐	
• LIGHTING CHECKED?	☐	
• WATER LEVEL CHECKED?	☐	
• CONDITIONER CHECKED?	☐	
• HEATER CHECKED?	☐	

ADDITIONAL NOTES	AQUASCAPE IDEAS & SKETCHES

DATE		WATER QUALITY	

DATE

TIME

TANK

WATER TYPE

WATER QUALITY

• TEMP	• % CHANGE
• PH LEVEL	• AMMONIA
• NITRITE	• NITRATE

FISH COUNT

FISHES ADDED

FISHES LOST

FISH BEHAVIOUR

LAZY   1   2   3   4   5   ACTIVE
◯   ◯   ◯   ◯   ◯

AQUARIUM CHECK LIST

GEAR / EQUIPMENT	TICK BOX	ADDITIONAL NOTES
FILTERS CHECKED?	☐	
PUMPS CHECKED?	☐	
TUBING CHECKED?	☐	
NET CHECKED?	☐	
LIGHTING CHECKED?	☐	
WATER LEVEL CHECKED?	☐	
CONDITIONER CHECKED?	☐	
HEATER CHECKED?	☐	

ADDITIONAL NOTES

AQUASCAPE IDEAS & SKETCHES

📅 **DATE**	💧 **WATER QUALITY**	
🕐 **TIME**	• TEMP	• % CHANGE
🐟 **TANK**	• PH LEVEL	• AMMONIA
🌊 **WATER TYPE**	• NITRITE	• NITRATE

FISH COUNT

FISHES ADDED

FISHES LOST

FISH BEHAVIOUR

LAZY 1 2 3 4 5 ACTIV

AQUARIUM CHECK LIST

🔧 GEAR / EQUIPMENT	☑ TICK BOX	✍ ADDITIONAL NOTES
• FILTERS CHECKED?	☐	
• PUMPS CHECKED?	☐	
• TUBING CHECKED?	☐	
• NET CHECKED?	☐	
• LIGHTING CHECKED?	☐	
• WATER LEVEL CHECKED?	☐	
• CONDITIONER CHECKED?	☐	
• HEATER CHECKED?	☐	

ADDITIONAL NOTES

AQUASCAPE IDEAS & SKETCHES

DATE	**WATER QUALITY**	
TIME	• TEMP	• % CHANGE
TANK	• PH LEVEL	• AMMONIA
WATER TYPE	• NITRITE	• NITRATE

FISH COUNT

FISHES ADDED

FISHES LOST

FISH BEHAVIOUR

	1	2	3	4	5	
LAZY ◯		◯	◯	◯	◯	ACTIVE

AQUARIUM CHECK LIST

GEAR / EQUIPMENT	TICK BOX	ADDITIONAL NOTES
FILTERS CHECKED?	☐	
PUMPS CHECKED?	☐	
TUBING CHECKED?	☐	
NET CHECKED?	☐	
LIGHTING CHECKED?	☐	
WATER LEVEL CHECKED?	☐	
CONDITIONER CHECKED?	☐	
HEATER CHECKED?	☐	

ADDITIONAL NOTES

AQUASCAPE IDEAS & SKETCHES

📅 **DATE**
🕐 **TIME**
🐠 **TANK**
〰️ **WATER TYPE**

💧 WATER QUALITY

• TEMP	• % CHANGE
• PH LEVEL	• AMMONIA
• NITRITE	• NITRATE

🐟 **FISH COUNT**
🐠 **FISHES ADDED**
🐟 **FISHES LOST**

FISH BEHAVIOUR

🐠 LAZY 1 ◯ 2 ◯ 3 ◯ 4 ◯ 5 ◯ ACTIV 🐟

AQUARIUM CHECK LIST

🔧 GEAR / EQUIPMENT	☑️ TICK BOX	📝 ADDITIONAL NOTES
• FILTERS CHECKED?	☐	
• PUMPS CHECKED?	☐	
• TUBING CHECKED?	☐	
• NET CHECKED?	☐	
• LIGHTING CHECKED?	☐	
• WATER LEVEL CHECKED?	☐	
• CONDITIONER CHECKED?	☐	
• HEATER CHECKED?	☐	

ADDITIONAL NOTES

AQUASCAPE IDEAS & SKETCHES

DATE

TIME

TANK

WATER TYPE

WATER QUALITY

• TEMP	• % CHANGE
• PH LEVEL	• AMMONIA
• NITRITE	• NITRATE

FISH COUNT

FISHES ADDED

FISHES LOST

FISH BEHAVIOUR

LAZY 1 2 3 4 5 ACTIVE

AQUARIUM CHECK LIST

GEAR / EQUIPMENT	TICK BOX	ADDITIONAL NOTES
FILTERS CHECKED?	☐	
PUMPS CHECKED?	☐	
TUBING CHECKED?	☐	
NET CHECKED?	☐	
LIGHTING CHECKED?	☐	
WATER LEVEL CHECKED?	☐	
CONDITIONER CHECKED?	☐	
HEATER CHECKED?	☐	

ADDITIONAL NOTES

AQUASCAPE IDEAS & SKETCHES

DATE

TIME

TANK

WATER TYPE

WATER QUALITY

• TEMP	• % CHANGE
• PH LEVEL	• AMMONIA
• NITRITE	• NITRATE

FISH COUNT

FISHES ADDED

FISHES LOST

FISH BEHAVIOUR

LAZY 1 2 3 4 5 ACTIV

AQUARIUM CHECK LIST

GEAR / EQUIPMENT	TICK BOX	ADDITIONAL NOTES
• FILTERS CHECKED?	☐	
• PUMPS CHECKED?	☐	
• TUBING CHECKED?	☐	
• NET CHECKED?	☐	
• LIGHTING CHECKED?	☐	
• WATER LEVEL CHECKED?	☐	
• CONDITIONER CHECKED?	☐	
• HEATER CHECKED?	☐	

ADDITIONAL NOTES

AQUASCAPE IDEAS & SKETCHES

DATE

TIME

TANK

WATER TYPE

WATER QUALITY

• TEMP	• % CHANGE
• PH LEVEL	• AMMONIA
• NITRITE	• NITRATE

FISH COUNT

FISHES ADDED

FISHES LOST

FISH BEHAVIOUR

LAZY 1 ◯ 2 ◯ 3 ◯ 4 ◯ 5 ◯ ACTIVE

AQUARIUM CHECK LIST

GEAR / EQUIPMENT	TICK BOX	ADDITIONAL NOTES
FILTERS CHECKED?	☐	
PUMPS CHECKED?	☐	
TUBING CHECKED?	☐	
NET CHECKED?	☐	
LIGHTING CHECKED?	☐	
WATER LEVEL CHECKED?	☐	
CONDITIONER CHECKED?	☐	
HEATER CHECKED?	☐	

ADDITIONAL NOTES

AQUASCAPE IDEAS & SKETCHES

📅 **DATE**	💧 **WATER QUALITY**	
🕐 **TIME**	• TEMP	• % CHANGE
🐠 **TANK**	• PH LEVEL	• AMMONIA
🌊 **WATER TYPE**	• NITRITE	• NITRATE

🐠 **FISH COUNT**
🐟 **FISHES ADDED**
🐟 **FISHES LOST**

FISH BEHAVIOUR

🐠 1 2 3 4 5 🐟
LAZY ○ ○ ○ ○ ○ ACTIV

AQUARIUM CHECK LIST

🔧 GEAR / EQUIPMENT	☑ TICK BOX	📝 ADDITIONAL NOTES
• FILTERS CHECKED?	☐	
• PUMPS CHECKED?	☐	
• TUBING CHECKED?	☐	
• NET CHECKED?	☐	
• LIGHTING CHECKED?	☐	
• WATER LEVEL CHECKED?	☐	
• CONDITIONER CHECKED?	☐	
• HEATER CHECKED?	☐	

ADDITIONAL NOTES

AQUASCAPE IDEAS & SKETCHES

DATE		WATER QUALITY	

DATE

TIME

TANK

WATER TYPE

WATER QUALITY

• TEMP	• % CHANGE
• PH LEVEL	• AMMONIA
• NITRITE	• NITRATE

FISH COUNT

FISHES ADDED

FISHES LOST

FISH BEHAVIOUR

	1	2	3	4	5	
LAZY	○	○	○	○	○	ACTIVE

AQUARIUM CHECK LIST

GEAR / EQUIPMENT	TICK BOX	ADDITIONAL NOTES
FILTERS CHECKED?	☐	
PUMPS CHECKED?	☐	
TUBING CHECKED?	☐	
NET CHECKED?	☐	
LIGHTING CHECKED?	☐	
WATER LEVEL CHECKED?	☐	
CONDITIONER CHECKED?	☐	
HEATER CHECKED?	☐	

ADDITIONAL NOTES

AQUASCAPE IDEAS & SKETCHES

📅 DATE		☀️ WATER QUALITY	
🕐 TIME		• TEMP	• % CHANGE
🐠 TANK		• PH LEVEL	• AMMONIA
〰️ WATER TYPE		• NITRITE	• NITRATE

🐠 FISH COUNT
🐠 FISHES ADDED
🐟 FISHES LOST

FISH BEHAVIOUR

🐠 LAZY 1 ○ 2 ○ 3 ○ 4 ○ 5 ○ ACTIVE 🐟

AQUARIUM CHECK LIST

🔧 GEAR / EQUIPMENT	☑️ TICK BOX	📝 ADDITIONAL NOTES
• FILTERS CHECKED?	☐	
• PUMPS CHECKED?	☐	
• TUBING CHECKED?	☐	
• NET CHECKED?	☐	
• LIGHTING CHECKED?	☐	
• WATER LEVEL CHECKED?	☐	
• CONDITIONER CHECKED?	☐	
• HEATER CHECKED?	☐	

ADDITIONAL NOTES

AQUASCAPE IDEAS & SKETCHES

DATE

TIME

TANK

WATER TYPE

:☼: WATER QUALITY

• TEMP	• % CHANGE
• PH LEVEL	• AMMONIA
• NITRITE	• NITRATE

FISH COUNT

FISHES ADDED

FISHES LOST

FISH BEHAVIOUR

LAZY ○ 1 ○ 2 ○ 3 ○ 4 ○ 5 ACTIVE

AQUARIUM CHECK LIST

GEAR / EQUIPMENT	TICK BOX	ADDITIONAL NOTES
FILTERS CHECKED?	☐	
PUMPS CHECKED?	☐	
TUBING CHECKED?	☐	
NET CHECKED?	☐	
LIGHTING CHECKED?	☐	
WATER LEVEL CHECKED?	☐	
CONDITIONER CHECKED?	☐	
HEATER CHECKED?	☐	

ADDITIONAL NOTES

AQUASCAPE IDEAS & SKETCHES

📅 DATE		:💧: WATER QUALITY	
🕐 TIME		• TEMP	• % CHANGE
🐟 TANK		• PH LEVEL	• AMMONIA
🌊 WATER TYPE		• NITRITE	• NITRATE

🐠 FISH COUNT
🐟 FISHES ADDED
🐟 FISHES LOST

FISH BEHAVIOUR

🐟   1   2   3   4   5   🐟

LAZY ⭕   ⭕   ⭕   ⭕   ⭕ ACTIV

AQUARIUM CHECK LIST

🔧 GEAR / EQUIPMENT	☑ TICK BOX	📝 ADDITIONAL NOTES
• FILTERS CHECKED?	☐	
• PUMPS CHECKED?	☐	
• TUBING CHECKED?	☐	
• NET CHECKED?	☐	
• LIGHTING CHECKED?	☐	
• WATER LEVEL CHECKED?	☐	
• CONDITIONER CHECKED?	☐	
• HEATER CHECKED?	☐	

ADDITIONAL NOTES	AQUASCAPE IDEAS & SKETCHES

DATE		WATER QUALITY	

DATE

TIME

TANK

WATER TYPE

WATER QUALITY

• TEMP	• % CHANGE
• PH LEVEL	• AMMONIA
• NITRITE	• NITRATE

FISH COUNT

FISHES ADDED

FISHES LOST

FISH BEHAVIOUR

LAZY 1 2 3 4 5 ACTIVE

AQUARIUM CHECK LIST

GEAR / EQUIPMENT	TICK BOX	ADDITIONAL NOTES
FILTERS CHECKED?	☐	
PUMPS CHECKED?	☐	
TUBING CHECKED?	☐	
NET CHECKED?	☐	
LIGHTING CHECKED?	☐	
WATER LEVEL CHECKED?	☐	
CONDITIONER CHECKED?	☐	
HEATER CHECKED?	☐	

ADDITIONAL NOTES

AQUASCAPE IDEAS & SKETCHES

📅 DATE		💧 WATER QUALITY	
🕐 TIME		• TEMP	• % CHANGE
🐠 TANK		• PH LEVEL	• AMMONIA
🌊 WATER TYPE		• NITRITE	• NITRATE

🐠 FISH COUNT
🐠 FISHES ADDED
🐟 FISHES LOST

FISH BEHAVIOUR

🐠   1   2   3   4   5   🐟

LAZY ◯   ◯   ◯   ◯   ◯ ACTIV

AQUARIUM CHECK LIST

🔧 GEAR / EQUIPMENT	☑ TICK BOX	✏ ADDITIONAL NOTES
• FILTERS CHECKED?	☐	
• PUMPS CHECKED?	☐	
• TUBING CHECKED?	☐	
• NET CHECKED?	☐	
• LIGHTING CHECKED?	☐	
• WATER LEVEL CHECKED?	☐	
• CONDITIONER CHECKED?	☐	
• HEATER CHECKED?	☐	

ADDITIONAL NOTES

AQUASCAPE IDEAS & SKETCHES

DATE

TIME

TANK

WATER TYPE

WATER QUALITY

• TEMP	• % CHANGE
• PH LEVEL	• AMMONIA
• NITRITE	• NITRATE

FISH COUNT

FISHES ADDED

FISHES LOST

FISH BEHAVIOUR

LAZY 1 2 3 4 5 ACTIVE

AQUARIUM CHECK LIST

GEAR / EQUIPMENT	TICK BOX	ADDITIONAL NOTES
FILTERS CHECKED?	☐	
PUMPS CHECKED?	☐	
TUBING CHECKED?	☐	
NET CHECKED?	☐	
LIGHTING CHECKED?	☐	
WATER LEVEL CHECKED?	☐	
CONDITIONER CHECKED?	☐	
HEATER CHECKED?	☐	

ADDITIONAL NOTES

AQUASCAPE IDEAS & SKETCHES

DATE		WATER QUALITY	
TIME		• TEMP	• % CHANGE
TANK		• PH LEVEL	• AMMONIA
WATER TYPE		• NITRITE	• NITRATE

FISH COUNT
FISHES ADDED
FISHES LOST

FISH BEHAVIOUR

LAZY 1   2   3   4   5 ACTIVE

AQUARIUM CHECK LIST

GEAR / EQUIPMENT	TICK BOX	ADDITIONAL NOTES
• FILTERS CHECKED?	☐	
• PUMPS CHECKED?	☐	
• TUBING CHECKED?	☐	
• NET CHECKED?	☐	
• LIGHTING CHECKED?	☐	
• WATER LEVEL CHECKED?	☐	
• CONDITIONER CHECKED?	☐	
• HEATER CHECKED?	☐	

ADDITIONAL NOTES

AQUASCAPE IDEAS & SKETCHES

DATE		WATER QUALITY	

DATE

TIME

TANK

WATER TYPE

WATER QUALITY

• TEMP		• % CHANGE	
• PH LEVEL		• AMMONIA	
• NITRITE		• NITRATE	

FISH COUNT

FISHES ADDED

FISHES LOST

FISH BEHAVIOUR

	1	2	3	4	5	
LAZY	◯	◯	◯	◯	◯	ACTIVE

AQUARIUM CHECK LIST

GEAR / EQUIPMENT	TICK BOX	ADDITIONAL NOTES
FILTERS CHECKED?	☐	
PUMPS CHECKED?	☐	
TUBING CHECKED?	☐	
NET CHECKED?	☐	
LIGHTING CHECKED?	☐	
WATER LEVEL CHECKED?	☐	
CONDITIONER CHECKED?	☐	
HEATER CHECKED?	☐	

ADDITIONAL NOTES

AQUASCAPE IDEAS & SKETCHES

DATE

TIME

TANK

WATER TYPE

WATER QUALITY

• TEMP	• % CHANGE
• PH LEVEL	• AMMONIA
• NITRITE	• NITRATE

FISH COUNT

FISHES ADDED

FISHES LOST

FISH BEHAVIOUR

	1	2	3	4	5	
LAZY	○	○	○	○	○	ACTIV

AQUARIUM CHECK LIST

GEAR / EQUIPMENT	TICK BOX	ADDITIONAL NOTES
• FILTERS CHECKED?	☐	
• PUMPS CHECKED?	☐	
• TUBING CHECKED?	☐	
• NET CHECKED?	☐	
• LIGHTING CHECKED?	☐	
• WATER LEVEL CHECKED?	☐	
• CONDITIONER CHECKED?	☐	
• HEATER CHECKED?	☐	

ADDITIONAL NOTES

AQUASCAPE IDEAS & SKETCHES

DATE

TIME

TANK

WATER TYPE

WATER QUALITY

• TEMP		• % CHANGE	
• PH LEVEL		• AMMONIA	
• NITRITE		• NITRATE	

FISH COUNT

FISHES ADDED

FISHES LOST

FISH BEHAVIOUR

LAZY   1   2   3   4   5   ACTIVE

AQUARIUM CHECK LIST

GEAR / EQUIPMENT	TICK BOX	ADDITIONAL NOTES
FILTERS CHECKED?	☐	
PUMPS CHECKED?	☐	
TUBING CHECKED?	☐	
NET CHECKED?	☐	
LIGHTING CHECKED?	☐	
WATER LEVEL CHECKED?	☐	
CONDITIONER CHECKED?	☐	
HEATER CHECKED?	☐	

ADDITIONAL NOTES

AQUASCAPE IDEAS & SKETCHES

📅 **DATE**	⬦ **WATER QUALITY**	
🕐 **TIME**	• TEMP	• % CHANGE
🐟 **TANK**	• PH LEVEL	• AMMONIA
🌊 **WATER TYPE**	• NITRITE	• NITRATE

🐠 **FISH COUNT**
🐟 **FISHES ADDED**
⊲⪤⪥ **FISHES LOST**

FISH BEHAVIOUR

🐟 LAZY   1 ◯   2 ◯   3 ◯   4 ◯   5 ◯ 🐟 ACTIV

AQUARIUM CHECK LIST

🔧 GEAR / EQUIPMENT	☰ TICK BOX	🖊 ADDITIONAL NOTES
• FILTERS CHECKED?	☐	
• PUMPS CHECKED?	☐	
• TUBING CHECKED?	☐	
• NET CHECKED?	☐	
• LIGHTING CHECKED?	☐	
• WATER LEVEL CHECKED?	☐	
• CONDITIONER CHECKED?	☐	
• HEATER CHECKED?	☐	

ADDITIONAL NOTES

AQUASCAPE IDEAS & SKETCHES

DATE

TIME

TANK

WATER TYPE

WATER QUALITY

• TEMP	• % CHANGE
• PH LEVEL	• AMMONIA
• NITRITE	• NITRATE

FISH COUNT

FISHES ADDED

FISHES LOST

FISH BEHAVIOUR

LAZY   1   2   3   4   5   ACTIVE

AQUARIUM CHECK LIST

GEAR / EQUIPMENT	TICK BOX	ADDITIONAL NOTES
• FILTERS CHECKED?	☐	
• PUMPS CHECKED?	☐	
• TUBING CHECKED?	☐	
• NET CHECKED?	☐	
• LIGHTING CHECKED?	☐	
• WATER LEVEL CHECKED?	☐	
• CONDITIONER CHECKED?	☐	
• HEATER CHECKED?	☐	

ADDITIONAL NOTES

AQUASCAPE IDEAS & SKETCHES

DATE	WATER QUALITY	
TIME	• TEMP	• % CHANGE
TANK	• PH LEVEL	• AMMONIA
WATER TYPE	• NITRITE	• NITRATE

FISH COUNT

FISHES ADDED

FISHES LOST

FISH BEHAVIOUR

LAZY 1 2 3 4 5 ACTIVE

AQUARIUM CHECK LIST

GEAR / EQUIPMENT	TICK BOX	ADDITIONAL NOTES
• FILTERS CHECKED?	☐	
• PUMPS CHECKED?	☐	
• TUBING CHECKED?	☐	
• NET CHECKED?	☐	
• LIGHTING CHECKED?	☐	
• WATER LEVEL CHECKED?	☐	
• CONDITIONER CHECKED?	☐	
• HEATER CHECKED?	☐	

ADDITIONAL NOTES

AQUASCAPE IDEAS & SKETCHES

DATE

TIME

TANK

WATER TYPE

WATER QUALITY

• TEMP	• % CHANGE
• PH LEVEL	• AMMONIA
• NITRITE	• NITRATE

FISH COUNT

FISHES ADDED

FISHES LOST

FISH BEHAVIOUR

LAZY   1   2   3   4   5   ACTIVE

AQUARIUM CHECK LIST

GEAR / EQUIPMENT	TICK BOX	ADDITIONAL NOTES
• FILTERS CHECKED?	☐	
• PUMPS CHECKED?	☐	
• TUBING CHECKED?	☐	
• NET CHECKED?	☐	
• LIGHTING CHECKED?	☐	
• WATER LEVEL CHECKED?	☐	
• CONDITIONER CHECKED?	☐	
• HEATER CHECKED?	☐	

ADDITIONAL NOTES

AQUASCAPE IDEAS & SKETCHES

DATE

TIME

TANK

WATER TYPE

WATER QUALITY

• TEMP	• % CHANGE
• PH LEVEL	• AMMONIA
• NITRITE	• NITRATE

FISH COUNT

FISHES ADDED

FISHES LOST

FISH BEHAVIOUR

LAZY   1   2   3   4   5   ACTIVE

AQUARIUM CHECK LIST

GEAR / EQUIPMENT	TICK BOX	ADDITIONAL NOTES
• FILTERS CHECKED?	☐	
• PUMPS CHECKED?	☐	
• TUBING CHECKED?	☐	
• NET CHECKED?	☐	
• LIGHTING CHECKED?	☐	
• WATER LEVEL CHECKED?	☐	
• CONDITIONER CHECKED?	☐	
• HEATER CHECKED?	☐	

ADDITIONAL NOTES

AQUASCAPE IDEAS & SKETCHES

DATE

TIME

TANK

WATER TYPE

WATER QUALITY

• TEMP	• % CHANGE
• PH LEVEL	• AMMONIA
• NITRITE	• NITRATE

FISH COUNT

FISHES ADDED

FISHES LOST

FISH BEHAVIOUR

LAZY 1 2 3 4 5 ACTIVE

AQUARIUM CHECK LIST

GEAR / EQUIPMENT	TICK BOX	ADDITIONAL NOTES
• FILTERS CHECKED?	☐	
• PUMPS CHECKED?	☐	
• TUBING CHECKED?	☐	
• NET CHECKED?	☐	
• LIGHTING CHECKED?	☐	
• WATER LEVEL CHECKED?	☐	
• CONDITIONER CHECKED?	☐	
• HEATER CHECKED?	☐	

ADDITIONAL NOTES

AQUASCAPE IDEAS & SKETCHES

📅 DATE		◌ WATER QUALITY	
🕐 TIME		• TEMP	• % CHANGE
🐠 TANK		• PH LEVEL	• AMMONIA
〰 WATER TYPE		• NITRITE	• NITRATE

🐟 FISH COUNT	
🐟 FISHES ADDED	
🐟 FISHES LOST	

FISH BEHAVIOUR

🐟 LAZY   1 ○   2 ○   3 ○   4 ○   5 ○   🐟 ACTIVE

AQUARIUM CHECK LIST

🔧 GEAR / EQUIPMENT	☑ TICK BOX	📝 ADDITIONAL NOTES
• FILTERS CHECKED?	☐	
• PUMPS CHECKED?	☐	
• TUBING CHECKED?	☐	
• NET CHECKED?	☐	
• LIGHTING CHECKED?	☐	
• WATER LEVEL CHECKED?	☐	
• CONDITIONER CHECKED?	☐	
• HEATER CHECKED?	☐	

ADDITIONAL NOTES	AQUASCAPE IDEAS & SKETCHES

DATE

TIME

TANK

WATER TYPE

WATER QUALITY

• TEMP	• % CHANGE
• PH LEVEL	• AMMONIA
• NITRITE	• NITRATE

FISH COUNT

FISHES ADDED

FISHES LOST

FISH BEHAVIOUR

LAZY 1   2   3   4   5 ACTIVE

AQUARIUM CHECK LIST

GEAR / EQUIPMENT	TICK BOX	ADDITIONAL NOTES
• FILTERS CHECKED?	☐	
• PUMPS CHECKED?	☐	
• TUBING CHECKED?	☐	
• NET CHECKED?	☐	
• LIGHTING CHECKED?	☐	
• WATER LEVEL CHECKED?	☐	
• CONDITIONER CHECKED?	☐	
• HEATER CHECKED?	☐	

ADDITIONAL NOTES

AQUASCAPE IDEAS & SKETCHES

DATE

TIME

TANK

WATER TYPE

WATER QUALITY

• TEMP	• % CHANGE
• PH LEVEL	• AMMONIA
• NITRITE	• NITRATE

FISH COUNT

FISHES ADDED

FISHES LOST

FISH BEHAVIOUR

LAZY 1 2 3 4 5 ACTIVE

AQUARIUM CHECK LIST

GEAR / EQUIPMENT	TICK BOX	ADDITIONAL NOTES
• FILTERS CHECKED?	☐	
• PUMPS CHECKED?	☐	
• TUBING CHECKED?	☐	
• NET CHECKED?	☐	
• LIGHTING CHECKED?	☐	
• WATER LEVEL CHECKED?	☐	
• CONDITIONER CHECKED?	☐	
• HEATER CHECKED?	☐	

ADDITIONAL NOTES

AQUASCAPE IDEAS & SKETCHES

DATE

TIME

TANK

WATER TYPE

WATER QUALITY

• TEMP	• % CHANGE
• PH LEVEL	• AMMONIA
• NITRITE	• NITRATE

FISH COUNT

FISHES ADDED

FISHES LOST

FISH BEHAVIOUR

LAZY 1   2   3   4   5 ACTIVE

AQUARIUM CHECK LIST

GEAR / EQUIPMENT	TICK BOX	ADDITIONAL NOTES
• FILTERS CHECKED?	☐	
• PUMPS CHECKED?	☐	
• TUBING CHECKED?	☐	
• NET CHECKED?	☐	
• LIGHTING CHECKED?	☐	
• WATER LEVEL CHECKED?	☐	
• CONDITIONER CHECKED?	☐	
• HEATER CHECKED?	☐	

ADDITIONAL NOTES

AQUASCAPE IDEAS & SKETCHES

📅 **DATE**		💧 **WATER QUALITY**	

DATE

TIME

TANK

WATER TYPE

WATER QUALITY

• TEMP	• % CHANGE
• PH LEVEL	• AMMONIA
• NITRITE	• NITRATE

FISH COUNT

FISHES ADDED

FISHES LOST

FISH BEHAVIOUR

LAZY 1 2 3 4 5 ACTIVE

AQUARIUM CHECK LIST

🔧 GEAR / EQUIPMENT	📋 TICK BOX	📝 ADDITIONAL NOTES
• FILTERS CHECKED?	☐	
• PUMPS CHECKED?	☐	
• TUBING CHECKED?	☐	
• NET CHECKED?	☐	
• LIGHTING CHECKED?	☐	
• WATER LEVEL CHECKED?	☐	
• CONDITIONER CHECKED?	☐	
• HEATER CHECKED?	☐	

ADDITIONAL NOTES

AQUASCAPE IDEAS & SKETCHES

DATE

TIME

TANK

WATER TYPE

WATER QUALITY

• TEMP	• % CHANGE
• PH LEVEL	• AMMONIA
• NITRITE	• NITRATE

FISH COUNT

FISHES ADDED

FISHES LOST

FISH BEHAVIOUR

LAZY 1 2 3 4 5 ACTIVE

AQUARIUM CHECK LIST

GEAR / EQUIPMENT	TICK BOX	ADDITIONAL NOTES
• FILTERS CHECKED?	☐	
• PUMPS CHECKED?	☐	
• TUBING CHECKED?	☐	
• NET CHECKED?	☐	
• LIGHTING CHECKED?	☐	
• WATER LEVEL CHECKED?	☐	
• CONDITIONER CHECKED?	☐	
• HEATER CHECKED?	☐	

ADDITIONAL NOTES

AQUASCAPE IDEAS & SKETCHES

📅 **DATE**	⏺ **WATER QUALITY**	
🕐 **TIME**	• TEMP	• % CHANGE
🐠 **TANK**	• PH LEVEL	• AMMONIA
〰 **WATER TYPE**	• NITRITE	• NITRATE

🐟 **FISH COUNT**
🐠 **FISHES ADDED**
🐟 **FISHES LOST**

FISH BEHAVIOUR

🐟 LAZY   1 ○   2 ○   3 ○   4 ○   5 ○ 🐠 ACTIVE

AQUARIUM CHECK LIST

🔧 GEAR / EQUIPMENT	☑ TICK BOX	📝 ADDITIONAL NOTES
• FILTERS CHECKED?	☐	
• PUMPS CHECKED?	☐	
• TUBING CHECKED?	☐	
• NET CHECKED?	☐	
• LIGHTING CHECKED?	☐	
• WATER LEVEL CHECKED?	☐	
• CONDITIONER CHECKED?	☐	
• HEATER CHECKED?	☐	

ADDITIONAL NOTES

AQUASCAPE IDEAS & SKETCHES

📅 **DATE**			💧 **WATER QUALITY**	

📅 **DATE**	
🕐 **TIME**	
🐟 **TANK**	
🌊 **WATER TYPE**	

WATER QUALITY

• TEMP	• % CHANGE
• PH LEVEL	• AMMONIA
• NITRITE	• NITRATE

🐟 **FISH COUNT**	
🐠 **FISHES ADDED**	
🐟 **FISHES LOST**	

FISH BEHAVIOUR

🐟 LAZY ○ 1 ○ 2 ○ 3 ○ 4 ○ 5 🐟 ACTIVE

AQUARIUM CHECK LIST

🔧 GEAR / EQUIPMENT	☑ TICK BOX	📝 ADDITIONAL NOTES
• FILTERS CHECKED?	☐	
• PUMPS CHECKED?	☐	
• TUBING CHECKED?	☐	
• NET CHECKED?	☐	
• LIGHTING CHECKED?	☐	
• WATER LEVEL CHECKED?	☐	
• CONDITIONER CHECKED?	☐	
• HEATER CHECKED?	☐	

ADDITIONAL NOTES

AQUASCAPE IDEAS & SKETCHES

DATE

TIME

TANK

WATER TYPE

WATER QUALITY

• TEMP	• % CHANGE
• PH LEVEL	• AMMONIA
• NITRITE	• NITRATE

FISH COUNT

FISHES ADDED

FISHES LOST

FISH BEHAVIOUR

LAZY 1 2 3 4 5 ACTIVE

AQUARIUM CHECK LIST

GEAR / EQUIPMENT	TICK BOX	ADDITIONAL NOTES
• FILTERS CHECKED?	☐	
• PUMPS CHECKED?	☐	
• TUBING CHECKED?	☐	
• NET CHECKED?	☐	
• LIGHTING CHECKED?	☐	
• WATER LEVEL CHECKED?	☐	
• CONDITIONER CHECKED?	☐	
• HEATER CHECKED?	☐	

ADDITIONAL NOTES

AQUASCAPE IDEAS & SKETCHES

DATE

TIME

TANK

WATER TYPE

WATER QUALITY

• TEMP	• % CHANGE
• PH LEVEL	• AMMONIA
• NITRITE	• NITRATE

FISH COUNT

FISHES ADDED

FISHES LOST

FISH BEHAVIOUR

LAZY 1 2 3 4 5 ACTIVE

AQUARIUM CHECK LIST

GEAR / EQUIPMENT	TICK BOX	ADDITIONAL NOTES
• FILTERS CHECKED?	☐	
• PUMPS CHECKED?	☐	
• TUBING CHECKED?	☐	
• NET CHECKED?	☐	
• LIGHTING CHECKED?	☐	
• WATER LEVEL CHECKED?	☐	
• CONDITIONER CHECKED?	☐	
• HEATER CHECKED?	☐	

ADDITIONAL NOTES

AQUASCAPE IDEAS & SKETCHES

DATE		WATER QUALITY	
TIME		TEMP	% CHANGE
TANK		PH LEVEL	AMMONIA
WATER TYPE		NITRITE	NITRATE

FISH COUNT
FISHES ADDED
FISHES LOST

FISH BEHAVIOUR

LAZY 1 2 3 4 5 ACTIVE

AQUARIUM CHECK LIST

GEAR / EQUIPMENT	TICK BOX	ADDITIONAL NOTES
• FILTERS CHECKED?	☐	
• PUMPS CHECKED?	☐	
• TUBING CHECKED?	☐	
• NET CHECKED?	☐	
• LIGHTING CHECKED?	☐	
• WATER LEVEL CHECKED?	☐	
• CONDITIONER CHECKED?	☐	
• HEATER CHECKED?	☐	

ADDITIONAL NOTES

AQUASCAPE IDEAS & SKETCHES

📅 **DATE**		💧 **WATER QUALITY**	

🕐 **TIME**

🐠 **TANK**

〰️ **WATER TYPE**

WATER QUALITY	
• TEMP	• % CHANGE
• PH LEVEL	• AMMONIA
• NITRITE	• NITRATE

🐠 **FISH COUNT**

🐠 **FISHES ADDED**

🐟 **FISHES LOST**

FISH BEHAVIOUR

🐠 LAZY   1 ◯   2 ◯   3 ◯   4 ◯   5 ◯   ACTIVE 🐠

AQUARIUM CHECK LIST

🔧 GEAR / EQUIPMENT	☑️ TICK BOX	📝 ADDITIONAL NOTES
• FILTERS CHECKED?	☐	
• PUMPS CHECKED?	☐	
• TUBING CHECKED?	☐	
• NET CHECKED?	☐	
• LIGHTING CHECKED?	☐	
• WATER LEVEL CHECKED?	☐	
• CONDITIONER CHECKED?	☐	
• HEATER CHECKED?	☐	

ADDITIONAL NOTES	**AQUASCAPE IDEAS & SKETCHES**

DATE		WATER QUALITY	
TIME		• TEMP	• % CHANGE
TANK		• PH LEVEL	• AMMONIA
WATER TYPE		• NITRITE	• NITRATE

FISH COUNT	
FISHES ADDED	
FISHES LOST	

FISH BEHAVIOUR

LAZY 1 2 3 4 5 ACTIVE

AQUARIUM CHECK LIST

GEAR / EQUIPMENT	TICK BOX	ADDITIONAL NOTES
• FILTERS CHECKED?	☐	
• PUMPS CHECKED?	☐	
• TUBING CHECKED?	☐	
• NET CHECKED?	☐	
• LIGHTING CHECKED?	☐	
• WATER LEVEL CHECKED?	☐	
• CONDITIONER CHECKED?	☐	
• HEATER CHECKED?	☐	

ADDITIONAL NOTES

AQUASCAPE IDEAS & SKETCHES

DATE

TIME

TANK

WATER TYPE

WATER QUALITY

TEMP	% CHANGE
PH LEVEL	AMMONIA
NITRITE	NITRATE

FISH COUNT

FISHES ADDED

FISHES LOST

FISH BEHAVIOUR

LAZY 1 2 3 4 5 ACTIVE

AQUARIUM CHECK LIST

GEAR / EQUIPMENT	TICK BOX	ADDITIONAL NOTES
• FILTERS CHECKED?	☐	
• PUMPS CHECKED?	☐	
• TUBING CHECKED?	☐	
• NET CHECKED?	☐	
• LIGHTING CHECKED?	☐	
• WATER LEVEL CHECKED?	☐	
• CONDITIONER CHECKED?	☐	
• HEATER CHECKED?	☐	

ADDITIONAL NOTES

AQUASCAPE IDEAS & SKETCHES

DATE		WATER QUALITY	
TIME		• TEMP	• % CHANGE
TANK		• PH LEVEL	• AMMONIA
WATER TYPE		• NITRITE	• NITRATE

FISH COUNT
FISHES ADDED
FISHES LOST

FISH BEHAVIOUR

LAZY 1 2 3 4 5 ACTIVE

AQUARIUM CHECK LIST

GEAR / EQUIPMENT	TICK BOX	ADDITIONAL NOTES
• FILTERS CHECKED?	☐	
• PUMPS CHECKED?	☐	
• TUBING CHECKED?	☐	
• NET CHECKED?	☐	
• LIGHTING CHECKED?	☐	
• WATER LEVEL CHECKED?	☐	
• CONDITIONER CHECKED?	☐	
• HEATER CHECKED?	☐	

ADDITIONAL NOTES

AQUASCAPE IDEAS & SKETCHES

DATE

TIME

TANK

WATER TYPE

WATER QUALITY

• TEMP	• % CHANGE
• PH LEVEL	• AMMONIA
• NITRITE	• NITRATE

FISH COUNT

FISHES ADDED

FISHES LOST

FISH BEHAVIOUR

LAZY 1 2 3 4 5 ACTIVE

AQUARIUM CHECK LIST

GEAR / EQUIPMENT	TICK BOX	ADDITIONAL NOTES
• FILTERS CHECKED?	☐	
• PUMPS CHECKED?	☐	
• TUBING CHECKED?	☐	
• NET CHECKED?	☐	
• LIGHTING CHECKED?	☐	
• WATER LEVEL CHECKED?	☐	
• CONDITIONER CHECKED?	☐	
• HEATER CHECKED?	☐	

ADDITIONAL NOTES

AQUASCAPE IDEAS & SKETCHES

DATE

TIME

TANK

WATER TYPE

WATER QUALITY

• TEMP	• % CHANGE
• PH LEVEL	• AMMONIA
• NITRITE	• NITRATE

FISH COUNT

FISHES ADDED

FISHES LOST

FISH BEHAVIOUR

1	2	3	4	5

LAZY ○ ○ ○ ○ ○ ACTIVE

AQUARIUM CHECK LIST

GEAR / EQUIPMENT	TICK BOX	ADDITIONAL NOTES
• FILTERS CHECKED?	☐	
• PUMPS CHECKED?	☐	
• TUBING CHECKED?	☐	
• NET CHECKED?	☐	
• LIGHTING CHECKED?	☐	
• WATER LEVEL CHECKED?	☐	
• CONDITIONER CHECKED?	☐	
• HEATER CHECKED?	☐	

ADDITIONAL NOTES

AQUASCAPE IDEAS & SKETCHES

DATE		WATER QUALITY	

DATE

TIME

TANK

WATER TYPE

WATER QUALITY

• TEMP	• % CHANGE
• PH LEVEL	• AMMONIA
• NITRITE	• NITRATE

FISH COUNT

FISHES ADDED

FISHES LOST

FISH BEHAVIOUR

LAZY	1	2	3	4	5	ACTIVE

AQUARIUM CHECK LIST

GEAR / EQUIPMENT	TICK BOX	ADDITIONAL NOTES
• FILTERS CHECKED?	☐	
• PUMPS CHECKED?	☐	
• TUBING CHECKED?	☐	
• NET CHECKED?	☐	
• LIGHTING CHECKED?	☐	
• WATER LEVEL CHECKED?	☐	
• CONDITIONER CHECKED?	☐	
• HEATER CHECKED?	☐	

ADDITIONAL NOTES

AQUASCAPE IDEAS & SKETCHES

DATE		WATER QUALITY	
TIME		• TEMP	• % CHANGE
TANK		• PH LEVEL	• AMMONIA
WATER TYPE		• NITRITE	• NITRATE

FISH COUNT		FISH BEHAVIOUR
FISHES ADDED		
FISHES LOST		

LAZY   1   2   3   4   5   ACTIVE

AQUARIUM CHECK LIST

GEAR / EQUIPMENT	TICK BOX	ADDITIONAL NOTES
• FILTERS CHECKED?	☐	
• PUMPS CHECKED?	☐	
• TUBING CHECKED?	☐	
• NET CHECKED?	☐	
• LIGHTING CHECKED?	☐	
• WATER LEVEL CHECKED?	☐	
• CONDITIONER CHECKED?	☐	
• HEATER CHECKED?	☐	

ADDITIONAL NOTES	AQUASCAPE IDEAS & SKETCHES

DATE		**WATER QUALITY**	
TIME		• TEMP	• % CHANGE
TANK		• PH LEVEL	• AMMONIA
WATER TYPE		• NITRITE	• NITRATE

FISH COUNT	**FISH BEHAVIOUR**
FISHES ADDED	LAZY 1 2 3 4 5 ACTIVE
FISHES LOST	

AQUARIUM CHECK LIST

GEAR / EQUIPMENT	TICK BOX	ADDITIONAL NOTES
• FILTERS CHECKED?	☐	
• PUMPS CHECKED?	☐	
• TUBING CHECKED?	☐	
• NET CHECKED?	☐	
• LIGHTING CHECKED?	☐	
• WATER LEVEL CHECKED?	☐	
• CONDITIONER CHECKED?	☐	
• HEATER CHECKED?	☐	

ADDITIONAL NOTES	**AQUASCAPE IDEAS & SKETCHES**

DATE

TIME

TANK

WATER TYPE

WATER QUALITY

• TEMP	• % CHANGE
• PH LEVEL	• AMMONIA
• NITRITE	• NITRATE

FISH COUNT

FISHES ADDED

FISHES LOST

FISH BEHAVIOUR

LAZY 1 2 3 4 5 ACTIVE

AQUARIUM CHECK LIST

GEAR / EQUIPMENT	TICK BOX	ADDITIONAL NOTES
• FILTERS CHECKED?	☐	
• PUMPS CHECKED?	☐	
• TUBING CHECKED?	☐	
• NET CHECKED?	☐	
• LIGHTING CHECKED?	☐	
• WATER LEVEL CHECKED?	☐	
• CONDITIONER CHECKED?	☐	
• HEATER CHECKED?	☐	

ADDITIONAL NOTES

AQUASCAPE IDEAS & SKETCHES

DATE

TIME

TANK

WATER TYPE

WATER QUALITY

• TEMP	• % CHANGE
• PH LEVEL	• AMMONIA
• NITRITE	• NITRATE

FISH COUNT

FISHES ADDED

FISHES LOST

FISH BEHAVIOUR

LAZY   1   2   3   4   5   ACTIVE

AQUARIUM CHECK LIST

GEAR / EQUIPMENT	TICK BOX	ADDITIONAL NOTES
• FILTERS CHECKED?	☐	
• PUMPS CHECKED?	☐	
• TUBING CHECKED?	☐	
• NET CHECKED?	☐	
• LIGHTING CHECKED?	☐	
• WATER LEVEL CHECKED?	☐	
• CONDITIONER CHECKED?	☐	
• HEATER CHECKED?	☐	

ADDITIONAL NOTES

AQUASCAPE IDEAS & SKETCHES

DATE

TIME

TANK

WATER TYPE

WATER QUALITY

• TEMP	• % CHANGE
• PH LEVEL	• AMMONIA
• NITRITE	• NITRATE

FISH COUNT

FISHES ADDED

FISHES LOST

FISH BEHAVIOUR

LAZY 1 2 3 4 5 ACTIVE

AQUARIUM CHECK LIST

GEAR / EQUIPMENT	TICK BOX	ADDITIONAL NOTES
• FILTERS CHECKED?	☐	
• PUMPS CHECKED?	☐	
• TUBING CHECKED?	☐	
• NET CHECKED?	☐	
• LIGHTING CHECKED?	☐	
• WATER LEVEL CHECKED?	☐	
• CONDITIONER CHECKED?	☐	
• HEATER CHECKED?	☐	

ADDITIONAL NOTES

AQUASCAPE IDEAS & SKETCHES

DATE		WATER QUALITY	
TIME			
TANK		· TEMP	· % CHANGE
WATER TYPE		· PH LEVEL	· AMMONIA
		· NITRITE	· NITRATE

FISH COUNT	FISH BEHAVIOUR
FISHES ADDED	
FISHES LOST	LAZY 1 2 3 4 5 ACTIVE

AQUARIUM CHECK LIST

GEAR / EQUIPMENT	TICK BOX	ADDITIONAL NOTES
· FILTERS CHECKED?	☐	
· PUMPS CHECKED?	☐	
· TUBING CHECKED?	☐	
· NET CHECKED?	☐	
· LIGHTING CHECKED?	☐	
· WATER LEVEL CHECKED?	☐	
· CONDITIONER CHECKED?	☐	
· HEATER CHECKED?	☐	

ADDITIONAL NOTES

AQUASCAPE IDEAS & SKETCHES

DATE

TIME

TANK

WATER TYPE

WATER QUALITY

• TEMP	• % CHANGE
• PH LEVEL	• AMMONIA
• NITRITE	• NITRATE

FISH COUNT

FISHES ADDED

FISHES LOST

FISH BEHAVIOUR

LAZY   1   2   3   4   5   ACTIVE

AQUARIUM CHECK LIST

GEAR / EQUIPMENT	TICK BOX	ADDITIONAL NOTES
• FILTERS CHECKED?	☐	
• PUMPS CHECKED?	☐	
• TUBING CHECKED?	☐	
• NET CHECKED?	☐	
• LIGHTING CHECKED?	☐	
• WATER LEVEL CHECKED?	☐	
• CONDITIONER CHECKED?	☐	
• HEATER CHECKED?	☐	

ADDITIONAL NOTES

AQUASCAPE IDEAS & SKETCHES

DATE

TIME

TANK

WATER TYPE

WATER QUALITY

• TEMP	• % CHANGE
• PH LEVEL	• AMMONIA
• NITRITE	• NITRATE

FISH COUNT

FISHES ADDED

FISHES LOST

FISH BEHAVIOUR

LAZY   1   2   3   4   5   ACTIVE

AQUARIUM CHECK LIST

GEAR / EQUIPMENT	TICK BOX	ADDITIONAL NOTES
• FILTERS CHECKED?	☐	
• PUMPS CHECKED?	☐	
• TUBING CHECKED?	☐	
• NET CHECKED?	☐	
• LIGHTING CHECKED?	☐	
• WATER LEVEL CHECKED?	☐	
• CONDITIONER CHECKED?	☐	
• HEATER CHECKED?	☐	

ADDITIONAL NOTES

AQUASCAPE IDEAS & SKETCHES

	DATE		WATER QUALITY	
	TIME			

	DATE
🗓	**DATE**
🕐	**TIME**
🐟	**TANK**
〰	**WATER TYPE**

💧 WATER QUALITY	
• TEMP	• % CHANGE
• PH LEVEL	• AMMONIA
• NITRITE	• NITRATE

🐠	**FISH COUNT**
🐟	**FISHES ADDED**
🐟	**FISHES LOST**

FISH BEHAVIOUR

🐟 LAZY   1 ○   2 ○   3 ○   4 ○   5 ○   🐟 ACTIVE

AQUARIUM CHECK LIST

🔧 GEAR / EQUIPMENT	☑ TICK BOX	✏ ADDITIONAL NOTES
• FILTERS CHECKED?	☐	
• PUMPS CHECKED?	☐	
• TUBING CHECKED?	☐	
• NET CHECKED?	☐	
• LIGHTING CHECKED?	☐	
• WATER LEVEL CHECKED?	☐	
• CONDITIONER CHECKED?	☐	
• HEATER CHECKED?	☐	

ADDITIONAL NOTES	AQUASCAPE IDEAS & SKETCHES

DATE

TIME

TANK

WATER TYPE

WATER QUALITY

• TEMP	• % CHANGE
• PH LEVEL	• AMMONIA
• NITRITE	• NITRATE

FISH COUNT

FISHES ADDED

FISHES LOST

FISH BEHAVIOUR

LAZY 1 2 3 4 5 ACTIVE

AQUARIUM CHECK LIST

GEAR / EQUIPMENT	TICK BOX	ADDITIONAL NOTES
• FILTERS CHECKED?	☐	
• PUMPS CHECKED?	☐	
• TUBING CHECKED?	☐	
• NET CHECKED?	☐	
• LIGHTING CHECKED?	☐	
• WATER LEVEL CHECKED?	☐	
• CONDITIONER CHECKED?	☐	
• HEATER CHECKED?	☐	

ADDITIONAL NOTES

AQUASCAPE IDEAS & SKETCHES

DATE

TIME

TANK

WATER TYPE

WATER QUALITY

• TEMP	• % CHANGE
• PH LEVEL	• AMMONIA
• NITRITE	• NITRATE

FISH COUNT

FISHES ADDED

FISHES LOST

FISH BEHAVIOUR

LAZY   1   2   3   4   5   ACTIVE

AQUARIUM CHECK LIST

GEAR / EQUIPMENT	TICK BOX	ADDITIONAL NOTES
• FILTERS CHECKED?	☐	
• PUMPS CHECKED?	☐	
• TUBING CHECKED?	☐	
• NET CHECKED?	☐	
• LIGHTING CHECKED?	☐	
• WATER LEVEL CHECKED?	☐	
• CONDITIONER CHECKED?	☐	
• HEATER CHECKED?	☐	

ADDITIONAL NOTES

AQUASCAPE IDEAS & SKETCHES

DATE

TIME

TANK

WATER TYPE

WATER QUALITY

• TEMP	• % CHANGE
• PH LEVEL	• AMMONIA
• NITRITE	• NITRATE

FISH COUNT

FISHES ADDED

FISHES LOST

FISH BEHAVIOUR

LAZY 1 2 3 4 5 ACTIVE

AQUARIUM CHECK LIST

GEAR / EQUIPMENT	TICK BOX	ADDITIONAL NOTES
• FILTERS CHECKED?	☐	
• PUMPS CHECKED?	☐	
• TUBING CHECKED?	☐	
• NET CHECKED?	☐	
• LIGHTING CHECKED?	☐	
• WATER LEVEL CHECKED?	☐	
• CONDITIONER CHECKED?	☐	
• HEATER CHECKED?	☐	

ADDITIONAL NOTES

AQUASCAPE IDEAS & SKETCHES

DATE

TIME

TANK

WATER TYPE

WATER QUALITY

• TEMP	• % CHANGE
• PH LEVEL	• AMMONIA
• NITRITE	• NITRATE

FISH COUNT

FISHES ADDED

FISHES LOST

FISH BEHAVIOUR

LAZY 1 2 3 4 5 ACTIVE

AQUARIUM CHECK LIST

GEAR / EQUIPMENT	TICK BOX	ADDITIONAL NOTES
• FILTERS CHECKED?	☐	
• PUMPS CHECKED?	☐	
• TUBING CHECKED?	☐	
• NET CHECKED?	☐	
• LIGHTING CHECKED?	☐	
• WATER LEVEL CHECKED?	☐	
• CONDITIONER CHECKED?	☐	
• HEATER CHECKED?	☐	

ADDITIONAL NOTES

AQUASCAPE IDEAS & SKETCHES

DATE

TIME

TANK

WATER TYPE

WATER QUALITY

• TEMP	• % CHANGE
• PH LEVEL	• AMMONIA
• NITRITE	• NITRATE

FISH COUNT

FISHES ADDED

FISHES LOST

FISH BEHAVIOUR

LAZY 1   2   3   4   5 ACTIVE

AQUARIUM CHECK LIST

GEAR / EQUIPMENT	TICK BOX	ADDITIONAL NOTES
• FILTERS CHECKED?	☐	
• PUMPS CHECKED?	☐	
• TUBING CHECKED?	☐	
• NET CHECKED?	☐	
• LIGHTING CHECKED?	☐	
• WATER LEVEL CHECKED?	☐	
• CONDITIONER CHECKED?	☐	
• HEATER CHECKED?	☐	

ADDITIONAL NOTES

AQUASCAPE IDEAS & SKETCHES

DATE		WATER QUALITY	
TIME		TEMP	% CHANGE
TANK		PH LEVEL	AMMONIA
WATER TYPE		NITRITE	NITRATE

FISH COUNT	FISH BEHAVIOUR
FISHES ADDED	
FISHES LOST	LAZY 1 2 3 4 5 ACTIVE

AQUARIUM CHECK LIST

GEAR / EQUIPMENT	TICK BOX	ADDITIONAL NOTES
• FILTERS CHECKED?	☐	
• PUMPS CHECKED?	☐	
• TUBING CHECKED?	☐	
• NET CHECKED?	☐	
• LIGHTING CHECKED?	☐	
• WATER LEVEL CHECKED?	☐	
• CONDITIONER CHECKED?	☐	
• HEATER CHECKED?	☐	

ADDITIONAL NOTES

AQUASCAPE IDEAS & SKETCHES

DATE

TIME

TANK

WATER TYPE

WATER QUALITY

• TEMP	• % CHANGE
• PH LEVEL	• AMMONIA
• NITRITE	• NITRATE

FISH COUNT

FISHES ADDED

FISHES LOST

FISH BEHAVIOUR

LAZY 1 ◯ 2 ◯ 3 ◯ 4 ◯ 5 ◯ ACTIVE

AQUARIUM CHECK LIST

GEAR / EQUIPMENT	TICK BOX	ADDITIONAL NOTES
• FILTERS CHECKED?	☐	
• PUMPS CHECKED?	☐	
• TUBING CHECKED?	☐	
• NET CHECKED?	☐	
• LIGHTING CHECKED?	☐	
• WATER LEVEL CHECKED?	☐	
• CONDITIONER CHECKED?	☐	
• HEATER CHECKED?	☐	

ADDITIONAL NOTES

AQUASCAPE IDEAS & SKETCHES

DATE

TIME

TANK

WATER TYPE

WATER QUALITY

• TEMP	• % CHANGE
• PH LEVEL	• AMMONIA
• NITRITE	• NITRATE

FISH COUNT

FISHES ADDED

FISHES LOST

FISH BEHAVIOUR

LAZY 1 2 3 4 5 ACTIVE

AQUARIUM CHECK LIST

GEAR / EQUIPMENT	TICK BOX	ADDITIONAL NOTES
• FILTERS CHECKED?	☐	
• PUMPS CHECKED?	☐	
• TUBING CHECKED?	☐	
• NET CHECKED?	☐	
• LIGHTING CHECKED?	☐	
• WATER LEVEL CHECKED?	☐	
• CONDITIONER CHECKED?	☐	
• HEATER CHECKED?	☐	

ADDITIONAL NOTES

AQUASCAPE IDEAS & SKETCHES

DATE

TIME

TANK

WATER TYPE

WATER QUALITY

• TEMP	• % CHANGE
• PH LEVEL	• AMMONIA
• NITRITE	• NITRATE

FISH COUNT

FISHES ADDED

FISHES LOST

FISH BEHAVIOUR

LAZY   1   2   3   4   5   ACTIVE

AQUARIUM CHECK LIST

GEAR / EQUIPMENT	TICK BOX	ADDITIONAL NOTES
• FILTERS CHECKED?	☐	
• PUMPS CHECKED?	☐	
• TUBING CHECKED?	☐	
• NET CHECKED?	☐	
• LIGHTING CHECKED?	☐	
• WATER LEVEL CHECKED?	☐	
• CONDITIONER CHECKED?	☐	
• HEATER CHECKED?	☐	

ADDITIONAL NOTES

AQUASCAPE IDEAS & SKETCHES

DATE		WATER QUALITY	
TIME		• TEMP	• % CHANGE
TANK		• PH LEVEL	• AMMONIA
WATER TYPE		• NITRITE	• NITRATE

FISH COUNT
FISHES ADDED
FISHES LOST

FISH BEHAVIOUR

LAZY   1   2   3   4   5   ACTIVE

AQUARIUM CHECK LIST

GEAR / EQUIPMENT	TICK BOX	ADDITIONAL NOTES
• FILTERS CHECKED?	☐	
• PUMPS CHECKED?	☐	
• TUBING CHECKED?	☐	
• NET CHECKED?	☐	
• LIGHTING CHECKED?	☐	
• WATER LEVEL CHECKED?	☐	
• CONDITIONER CHECKED?	☐	
• HEATER CHECKED?	☐	

ADDITIONAL NOTES

AQUASCAPE IDEAS & SKETCHES

DATE

TIME

TANK

WATER TYPE

WATER QUALITY

• TEMP	• % CHANGE
• PH LEVEL	• AMMONIA
• NITRITE	• NITRATE

FISH COUNT

FISHES ADDED

FISHES LOST

FISH BEHAVIOUR

LAZY 1 2 3 4 5 ACTIVE

AQUARIUM CHECK LIST

GEAR / EQUIPMENT	TICK BOX	ADDITIONAL NOTES
• FILTERS CHECKED?	☐	
• PUMPS CHECKED?	☐	
• TUBING CHECKED?	☐	
• NET CHECKED?	☐	
• LIGHTING CHECKED?	☐	
• WATER LEVEL CHECKED?	☐	
• CONDITIONER CHECKED?	☐	
• HEATER CHECKED?	☐	

ADDITIONAL NOTES

AQUASCAPE IDEAS & SKETCHES

📅 DATE		💧 WATER QUALITY	
🕐 TIME		• TEMP	• % CHANGE
🐠 TANK		• PH LEVEL	• AMMONIA
〰️ WATER TYPE		• NITRITE	• NITRATE

🐠 FISH COUNT
🐠 FISHES ADDED
🐟 FISHES LOST

FISH BEHAVIOUR

🐠 LAZY   1 ⬡   2 ⬡   3 ⬡   4 ⬡   5 ⬡   🐠 ACTIVE

AQUARIUM CHECK LIST

⚙️ GEAR / EQUIPMENT	☑️ TICK BOX	📝 ADDITIONAL NOTES
• FILTERS CHECKED?	☐	
• PUMPS CHECKED?	☐	
• TUBING CHECKED?	☐	
• NET CHECKED?	☐	
• LIGHTING CHECKED?	☐	
• WATER LEVEL CHECKED?	☐	
• CONDITIONER CHECKED?	☐	
• HEATER CHECKED?	☐	

ADDITIONAL NOTES

AQUASCAPE IDEAS & SKETCHES

DATE

TIME

TANK

WATER TYPE

WATER QUALITY

• TEMP	• % CHANGE
• PH LEVEL	• AMMONIA
• NITRITE	• NITRATE

FISH COUNT

FISHES ADDED

FISHES LOST

FISH BEHAVIOUR

LAZY 1 2 3 4 5 ACTIVE

AQUARIUM CHECK LIST

GEAR / EQUIPMENT	TICK BOX	ADDITIONAL NOTES
• FILTERS CHECKED?	☐	
• PUMPS CHECKED?	☐	
• TUBING CHECKED?	☐	
• NET CHECKED?	☐	
• LIGHTING CHECKED?	☐	
• WATER LEVEL CHECKED?	☐	
• CONDITIONER CHECKED?	☐	
• HEATER CHECKED?	☐	

ADDITIONAL NOTES

AQUASCAPE IDEAS & SKETCHES

📅 DATE		⬡ WATER QUALITY	
🕐 TIME		• TEMP	• % CHANGE
🐠 TANK		• PH LEVEL	• AMMONIA
〰 WATER TYPE		• NITRITE	• NITRATE

🐟 FISH COUNT		FISH BEHAVIOUR	
🐟 FISHES ADDED			
🐟 FISHES LOST			

FISH BEHAVIOUR

🐟 LAZY   1 ○   2 ○   3 ○   4 ○   5 ○   ACTIVE 🐟

AQUARIUM CHECK LIST

🛠 GEAR / EQUIPMENT	☑ TICK BOX	📝 ADDITIONAL NOTES
• FILTERS CHECKED?	☐	
• PUMPS CHECKED?	☐	
• TUBING CHECKED?	☐	
• NET CHECKED?	☐	
• LIGHTING CHECKED?	☐	
• WATER LEVEL CHECKED?	☐	
• CONDITIONER CHECKED?	☐	
• HEATER CHECKED?	☐	

ADDITIONAL NOTES

AQUASCAPE IDEAS & SKETCHES

DATE

TIME

TANK

WATER TYPE

WATER QUALITY

• TEMP	• % CHANGE
• PH LEVEL	• AMMONIA
• NITRITE	• NITRATE

FISH COUNT

FISHES ADDED

FISHES LOST

FISH BEHAVIOUR

LAZY   1   2   3   4   5   ACTIVE

AQUARIUM CHECK LIST

GEAR / EQUIPMENT	TICK BOX	ADDITIONAL NOTES
• FILTERS CHECKED?	☐	
• PUMPS CHECKED?	☐	
• TUBING CHECKED?	☐	
• NET CHECKED?	☐	
• LIGHTING CHECKED?	☐	
• WATER LEVEL CHECKED?	☐	
• CONDITIONER CHECKED?	☐	
• HEATER CHECKED?	☐	

ADDITIONAL NOTES

AQUASCAPE IDEAS & SKETCHES

📅 DATE		☀️ WATER QUALITY	
🕐 TIME		• TEMP	• % CHANGE
🐠 TANK		• PH LEVEL	• AMMONIA
〰️ WATER TYPE		• NITRITE	• NITRATE

🐟 FISH COUNT	
🐠 FISHES ADDED	
🐟 FISHES LOST	

FISH BEHAVIOUR

🐟 LAZY 1 ○ 2 ○ 3 ○ 4 ○ 5 ○ ACTIVE

AQUARIUM CHECK LIST

🔧 GEAR / EQUIPMENT	☑️ TICK BOX	📝 ADDITIONAL NOTES
• FILTERS CHECKED?	☐	
• PUMPS CHECKED?	☐	
• TUBING CHECKED?	☐	
• NET CHECKED?	☐	
• LIGHTING CHECKED?	☐	
• WATER LEVEL CHECKED?	☐	
• CONDITIONER CHECKED?	☐	
• HEATER CHECKED?	☐	

ADDITIONAL NOTES	AQUASCAPE IDEAS & SKETCHES

DATE

TIME

TANK

WATER TYPE

WATER QUALITY

• TEMP	• % CHANGE
• PH LEVEL	• AMMONIA
• NITRITE	• NITRATE

FISH COUNT

FISHES ADDED

FISHES LOST

FISH BEHAVIOUR

LAZY 1 2 3 4 5 ACTIVE

AQUARIUM CHECK LIST

GEAR / EQUIPMENT	TICK BOX	ADDITIONAL NOTES
• FILTERS CHECKED?	☐	
• PUMPS CHECKED?	☐	
• TUBING CHECKED?	☐	
• NET CHECKED?	☐	
• LIGHTING CHECKED?	☐	
• WATER LEVEL CHECKED?	☐	
• CONDITIONER CHECKED?	☐	
• HEATER CHECKED?	☐	

ADDITIONAL NOTES

AQUASCAPE IDEAS & SKETCHES

DATE

TIME

TANK

WATER TYPE

WATER QUALITY

• TEMP	• % CHANGE
• PH LEVEL	• AMMONIA
• NITRITE	• NITRATE

FISH COUNT

FISHES ADDED

FISHES LOST

FISH BEHAVIOUR

LAZY   1   2   3   4   5   ACTIVE

AQUARIUM CHECK LIST

GEAR / EQUIPMENT	TICK BOX	ADDITIONAL NOTES
• FILTERS CHECKED?	☐	
• PUMPS CHECKED?	☐	
• TUBING CHECKED?	☐	
• NET CHECKED?	☐	
• LIGHTING CHECKED?	☐	
• WATER LEVEL CHECKED?	☐	
• CONDITIONER CHECKED?	☐	
• HEATER CHECKED?	☐	

ADDITIONAL NOTES

AQUASCAPE IDEAS & SKETCHES

DATE _____

TIME _____

TANK _____

WATER TYPE _____

WATER QUALITY

• TEMP	• % CHANGE
• PH LEVEL	• AMMONIA
• NITRITE	• NITRATE

FISH COUNT _____

FISHES ADDED _____

FISHES LOST _____

FISH BEHAVIOUR

LAZY 1 2 3 4 5 ACTIVE

AQUARIUM CHECK LIST

GEAR / EQUIPMENT	TICK BOX	ADDITIONAL NOTES
• FILTERS CHECKED?	☐	
• PUMPS CHECKED?	☐	
• TUBING CHECKED?	☐	
• NET CHECKED?	☐	
• LIGHTING CHECKED?	☐	
• WATER LEVEL CHECKED?	☐	
• CONDITIONER CHECKED?	☐	
• HEATER CHECKED?	☐	

ADDITIONAL NOTES

AQUASCAPE IDEAS & SKETCHES

📅 **DATE**		☀️ **WATER QUALITY**	
🕐 **TIME**		• TEMP	• % CHANGE
🐠 **TANK**		• PH LEVEL	• AMMONIA
〰️ **WATER TYPE**		• NITRITE	• NITRATE

🐟 **FISH COUNT**
🐠 **FISHES ADDED**
🐟 **FISHES LOST**

FISH BEHAVIOUR

🐟 LAZY   1 ⚪   2 ⚪   3 ⚪   4 ⚪   5 ⚪ 🐟 ACTIVE

AQUARIUM CHECK LIST

🔧 GEAR / EQUIPMENT	📋 TICK BOX	📝 ADDITIONAL NOTES
• FILTERS CHECKED?	☐	
• PUMPS CHECKED?	☐	
• TUBING CHECKED?	☐	
• NET CHECKED?	☐	
• LIGHTING CHECKED?	☐	
• WATER LEVEL CHECKED?	☐	
• CONDITIONER CHECKED?	☐	
• HEATER CHECKED?	☐	

ADDITIONAL NOTES	**AQUASCAPE IDEAS & SKETCHES**

DATE		WATER QUALITY	

DATE

TIME

TANK

WATER TYPE

WATER QUALITY

• TEMP	• % CHANGE
• PH LEVEL	• AMMONIA
• NITRITE	• NITRATE

FISH COUNT

FISHES ADDED

FISHES LOST

FISH BEHAVIOUR

LAZY 1 2 3 4 5 ACTIVE

AQUARIUM CHECK LIST

GEAR / EQUIPMENT	TICK BOX	ADDITIONAL NOTES
• FILTERS CHECKED?	☐	
• PUMPS CHECKED?	☐	
• TUBING CHECKED?	☐	
• NET CHECKED?	☐	
• LIGHTING CHECKED?	☐	
• WATER LEVEL CHECKED?	☐	
• CONDITIONER CHECKED?	☐	
• HEATER CHECKED?	☐	

ADDITIONAL NOTES

AQUASCAPE IDEAS & SKETCHES

📅 DATE		☀️ WATER QUALITY	
🕐 TIME		• TEMP	• % CHANGE
🐠 TANK		• PH LEVEL	• AMMONIA
〰️ WATER TYPE		• NITRITE	• NITRATE

🐟 FISH COUNT
🐠 FISHES ADDED
🐟 FISHES LOST

FISH BEHAVIOUR

🐟 LAZY 1 ○ 2 ○ 3 ○ 4 ○ 5 ○ 🐟 ACTIVE

AQUARIUM CHECK LIST

🔧 GEAR / EQUIPMENT	☑️ TICK BOX	📝 ADDITIONAL NOTES
• FILTERS CHECKED?	☐	
• PUMPS CHECKED?	☐	
• TUBING CHECKED?	☐	
• NET CHECKED?	☐	
• LIGHTING CHECKED?	☐	
• WATER LEVEL CHECKED?	☐	
• CONDITIONER CHECKED?	☐	
• HEATER CHECKED?	☐	

ADDITIONAL NOTES

AQUASCAPE IDEAS & SKETCHES

DATE		WATER QUALITY	

DATE	
TIME	
TANK	
WATER TYPE	

WATER QUALITY

• TEMP	• % CHANGE
• PH LEVEL	• AMMONIA
• NITRITE	• NITRATE

FISH COUNT	
FISHES ADDED	
FISHES LOST	

FISH BEHAVIOUR

LAZY 1 2 3 4 5 ACTIVE

AQUARIUM CHECK LIST

GEAR / EQUIPMENT	TICK BOX	ADDITIONAL NOTES
• FILTERS CHECKED?	☐	
• PUMPS CHECKED?	☐	
• TUBING CHECKED?	☐	
• NET CHECKED?	☐	
• LIGHTING CHECKED?	☐	
• WATER LEVEL CHECKED?	☐	
• CONDITIONER CHECKED?	☐	
• HEATER CHECKED?	☐	

ADDITIONAL NOTES

AQUASCAPE IDEAS & SKETCHES

📅 DATE		⬡ WATER QUALITY	
🕐 TIME		• TEMP	• % CHANGE
🐠 TANK		• PH LEVEL	• AMMONIA
🌊 WATER TYPE		• NITRITE	• NITRATE

🐟 FISH COUNT
🐠 FISHES ADDED
🐟 FISHES LOST

FISH BEHAVIOUR

🐟 LAZY   1 ◯   2 ◯   3 ◯   4 ◯   5 ◯ 🐟 ACTIVE

AQUARIUM CHECK LIST

🔧 GEAR / EQUIPMENT	☑ TICK BOX	📝 ADDITIONAL NOTES
• FILTERS CHECKED?	◻	
• PUMPS CHECKED?	◻	
• TUBING CHECKED?	◻	
• NET CHECKED?	◻	
• LIGHTING CHECKED?	◻	
• WATER LEVEL CHECKED?	◻	
• CONDITIONER CHECKED?	◻	
• HEATER CHECKED?	◻	

ADDITIONAL NOTES

AQUASCAPE IDEAS & SKETCHES

DATE

TIME

TANK

WATER TYPE

WATER QUALITY

• TEMP	• % CHANGE
• PH LEVEL	• AMMONIA
• NITRITE	• NITRATE

FISH COUNT

FISHES ADDED

FISHES LOST

FISH BEHAVIOUR

LAZY   1   2   3   4   5   ACTIVE

○ ○ ○ ○ ○

AQUARIUM CHECK LIST

GEAR / EQUIPMENT	TICK BOX	ADDITIONAL NOTES
• FILTERS CHECKED?	☐	
• PUMPS CHECKED?	☐	
• TUBING CHECKED?	☐	
• NET CHECKED?	☐	
• LIGHTING CHECKED?	☐	
• WATER LEVEL CHECKED?	☐	
• CONDITIONER CHECKED?	☐	
• HEATER CHECKED?	☐	

ADDITIONAL NOTES

AQUASCAPE IDEAS & SKETCHES

Imprint

©2020 by Weißhirsch

Michael Seidou
Weißhirsch
Fichtelbachstraße 18d
86153 Augsburg

Weißhirsch

Printed in Great Britain
by Amazon

31493624R00070